Clear Speech

From the Start

Basic Pronunciation and
Listening Comprehension
in North American English

2nd Edition

Judy B. Gilbert

CAMBRIDGE
UNIVERSITY PRESS

CAMBRIDGE UNIVERSITY PRESS
Cambridge, New York, Melbourne, Madrid, Cape Town,
Singapore, São Paulo, Delhi, Mexico City

Cambridge University Press
32 Avenue of the Americas, New York, NY 10013-2473, USA

www.cambridge.org
Information on this title: www.cambridge.org/9781107687158

© Cambridge University Press 2012

First published 2001
2nd printing 2013

Printed in Hong Kong, China, by Golden Cup Printing Company Limited

A catalog record for this publication is available from the British Library.

ISBN 978-1-107-68715-8 Student's Book
ISBN 978-1-107-60431-5 Teacher's Resource and Assessment Book
ISBN 978-1-107-61172-6 Class and Assessment Audio CDs

For a full list of components, visit www.cambridge.org/clearspeech

Art direction, book design, layout services, and photo research: Q2A/Bill Smith
Audio production: Richard LePage and Associates

Welcome to
Clear Speech
The world's favorite pronunciation series

Clear Speech From the Start offers a variety of tools for learning and practicing pronunciation.

With the **Student's Book** you can learn and practice how to:

▸ speak more clearly

▸ listen to other people more efficiently

▸ guess the pronunciation of written words

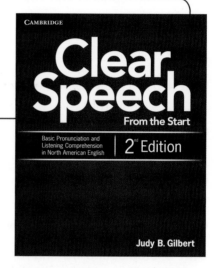

CAMBRIDGE

Clear Speech
From the Start

Basic Pronunciation and Listening Comprehension in North American English | 2ⁿᵈ Edition

Judy B. Gilbert

With the *Basic Pronunciation: Clear Speech From the Start* **App** for iPhone, iPad, and iPod touch available on the App Store, you can:

▸ play games and practice pronunciation in a fun interactive way

With the **Student's Book Audio** available at **www.cambridge.org/clearspeech**, you can:

▸ download the MP3s for all the listening activities in the Student's Book

▸ review and practice all the sounds and intonation and rhythm patterns presented and practiced in class

Contents

Appendices

Extra Practice 1
Vowels

Extra Practice 2
Problem Consonants

Scope and Sequence

Acknowledgments

Thanks to the following people for their contributions to the second edition of *Clear Speech From the Start:*

The reviewers Linda Bolet, Houston Community College, Texas; Katherine Chirinos, Houston Community College – Southwest, Texas; Nancy Hilty, College of Marin, California; Arlene Simmons, Los Angeles Unified School District, California; and Melissa Villamil, Houston Community College – Central, Texas.

My colleagues Barbara Bradford, Adam Brown, Madalena Cruz-Ferreira, Nancy Hilty, James Kirchner, Olle Kjellin, Barbara Seidlhofer, Michael Vaughan-Rees, and Robin Walker, for years of helping me think through fundamental linguistic and pedagogical issues.

Ellen Shaw for encouragement and guidance and for later pushing me to study what was known about spelling, so that students could be helped to guess how to pronounce the written word.

Judith Alderman, for drawing the pictures of the tongue shapes looking to the front; Dorothy Cribbs, for developing the original widened vowel font; Ames Kanemoto, for developing the concept of shrinking letters for continuants; and Jack Rummel, for his fine ragtime.

Karen Shimoda, Development Editor, who has been a much valued partner, helping solve the sequence and clarity issues that come with serious change; Debbie Goldblatt, Project Manager, for thoughtful review; Karen Brock, Senior Commissioning Editor, for her wisdom in decisions overseeing the development of both the book series and the apps; and Sheryl Olinsky Borg, Publishing Manager, and Maria Amélia Dalsenter, Managing Editor, for insightful supervision during the finishing phases of these books, to make them as easy to teach from as possible.

And to all those whose dedicated professionalism has helped shape this new edition of *Clear Speech From the Start.*

To Jerry, who fixes things.

Letter to the Teacher

For years before the first edition of this book, teachers had asked me to write a lower-level version of *Clear Speech*, the intermediate-level book of this series, because they felt that teaching pronunciation early would avoid fixed habits that are hard to overcome later. Students get discouraged when their efforts to communicate are misunderstood, so it is psychologically important to help them speak clearly from the beginning. This second edition of *Clear Speech From the Start* follows the same principles developed in the first edition but with new and improved features based on teacher recommendations.

The following pages of this letter outline the new features of the second edition and how they work with the six basic principles and approach of *Clear Speech From the Start*. The letter also provides suggestions for teaching the activities.

I hope that you find using this second edition of *Clear Speech From the Start* to be an enjoyable and professionally rewarding experience.

Judy B. Gilbert

New Features of *Clear Speech From the Start,* Second Edition

- **A pronunciation pyramid adds new support.** This concept makes it easier for students to understand how the various aspects of spoken English work together. The pyramid is divided into four levels, each with a distinctive color. The base, or foundation, level of the pyramid is the *word group* (a short sentence, a clause, or a phrase). Within that base, there is the *most important word*, which is the focus of the word group. Within the most important word, there is one *strong syllable*. The vowel at the center of this syllable is the *peak vowel*, which is the top of the pyramid and the peak of information. Accuracy is necessary when pronouncing this vowel.

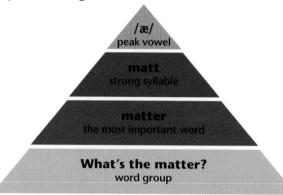

Throughout the book, the pyramid appears at appropriate points to remind students how the specific topic being taught fits into the whole system of spoken English. With the same purpose, Rules and Vowel Work boxes are shaded in the pyramid level color that corresponds to the topic being presented.

- **More support for vowel rules is given.** Sound symbols are used in specific tasks to help students recognize how pronunciation of sounds relates to the spelling rules.

- **Expanded appendices and extra practice are provided.** The back of the book now includes the original appendices with useful information and mouth diagrams and new sections for extra practice with vowels and "problem" consonants.

- **A four-color design adds visual appeal and clarity to presentation and practice.** A color design as well as updated illustrations and graphics make the presentations even clearer and provide more support for the practice tasks.

- **The audio program is available for students to download.** The complete audio program for the Student's Book is available as MP3s on the *Clear Speech* Website (www.cambridge.org/clearspeech). Students can now download the audio for further practice outside the classroom.

- **An App with games makes self-study practice more engaging.** Four games with hundreds of activities provide further practice of key pronunciation aspects. The app for iPhone, iPad, and iPod touch is available on the App Store.

Six Principles of *Clear Speech From the Start*

1 Topics that are the most important are taught first. This allows you to focus on the elements your students need most, such as how English speakers call attention to the most important words or which vowels need to be extra clear.

2 Teaching points are designed to help students with both listening comprehension and intelligibility. Tasks are presented with plenty of listening preparation before students are asked to speak. Words are presented both in regular spelled form and in special word boxes that show how they sound.

3 Spelling and phonics rules are presented to help students guess pronunciation. Vowel rule boxes provide the spelling and phonics rules adapted to English language students' needs. These rules can help students guess the pronunciation of unknown words and make them much more autonomous learners.

4 Visual and kinesthetic modes emphasize key points. For example, the lengthening of strong (stressed) vowels is presented in the following manner.

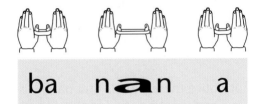

This makes the presentation clearer and more memorable for learners, especially visual and kinesthetic ones.

5 Signals of spoken English are combined into simple, memorable phrases and sentences. The Music of English boxes show these simple, yet common phrases and sentences, along with lines that illustrate the use of pitch for emphasis. Practice with these phrases and sentences help fix patterns in memory. A special color is used for these boxes, to indicate that all the levels of the pronunciation pyramid are being practiced at the same time.

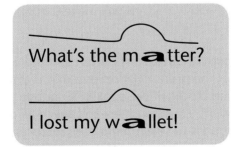

6 Student pair work is emphasized. This provides a communicative challenge and gives students the opportunity to practice not only speaking but also practice listening to different voices and pronunciations.

The *Clear Speech From the Start* Approach

The relationship between speaking and listening comprehension is made clear. Students who learn to recognize important signals of the natural rhythms and melodies of English often report improved understanding of speech on TV, in movies, and in face-to-face conversation.

English learners regularly complain, "Native speakers talk too fast." This often results from difficulty recognizing grammar signals: the plural ending of "book**s**"; the past tense ending of "calle**d**"; or the future tense in contractions like "I'**ll**." Learners also tend to miss the significance of signals of emphasis, such as the difference between "Did you want a **cup** of soup?" vs. "Did you want a cup of **soup**?" Another problem that slows down learner's listening comprehension is unawareness of signals of word grouping. For example, when a telephone number is grouped incorrectly, the listener may be unable to understand it. All of these signals make it difficult for learners to process incoming English efficiently and are addressed in this book.

Students learn how rhythm and melody are used as signals. In English, rhythm and melody serve as signals to help the listener follow the intentions of the speaker. These signals communicate emphasis and make clear the relationship between ideas so that listeners can readily identify these relationships and understand the speaker's meaning.

Learners typically do not notice these signals that native listeners count on to help them follow meaning in a conversation. As a result, conversational breakdowns occur. Emphasis that conveys the wrong meaning or word groups that either run together or break in inappropriate places make it difficult for the listener to follow the speaker's meaning. If the burden becomes too great, the listener simply stops listening. The principle of "helping the listener to follow," therefore, is a vital one. It is essential to helping students develop "listener-friendly" pronunciation.

Students are given rhythm training. It is not usually efficient to teach individual sounds without establishing some basic understanding of the English system of rhythm. People learning new languages tend to practice new sounds in the rhythm of their first language, and this makes it harder to get the target sounds right. Mastering the new rhythm will make it easier for students to say the new sounds clearly.

Template sentences provide students with simple and transferable patterns. The essence of the pronunciation pyramid is that all of the levels of the pyramid – the building blocks of the spoken language – work at the same time and are interdependent. However, we can't teach all of these elements simultaneously. The solution is to teach *template sentences* – the word group that forms the base of the pyramid. These template sentences are found in the Music of English boxes. When templates are solidly placed in long-term memory, they can serve as an accurate resource for analysis of specific aspects of a flowing piece of spoken English.

Choral repetition reinforces the templates. The best way to teach template sentences is through *quality repetition*. Repetition, a truly ancient teaching method, fell into disfavor decades ago because teachers felt that it was boring. Repetition practice can indeed be boring, but *quality* repetition creates a momentum that is the opposite of boring and gives the students confidence.

To practice quality repetition, students first need to hear the template a number of times – in varying ways (loud, soft, whisper, etc.) but always at a normal speed retaining all the melodic and rhythmic features of natural English. If the sentence is slowed down, it will tend to lose these essential features.

Choral response gives support to each speaker who, if speaking alone, might falter and lose the rhythm. The auditory support of choral sound and the strengthening effect of repetition give the students confidence and the satisfaction that they are mastering a useful template of spoken English.

Teaching the Activities in *Clear Speech From the Start*

Clear Speech From the Start was designed to be used in a wide range of teaching situations; therefore, you should feel free to choose those activities that are most appropriate for your students. You may also wish to shorten some activities if further practice is unnecessary.

Listening activities: Listening tasks such as "Which word do you hear?" and "Which word is different?" can help students learn to recognize particular sounds and stress patterns. When students practice hearing final sounds that make a grammar difference – for example, past tense such as "close**d**" or plural endings such as "book**s**" – both listening comprehension and pronunciation will improve.

Student pair work: The pair-work practice is particularly important, as it gives the students a great deal of realistic interactive speaking and listening. Pair work offers the immediate feedback so important to motivation. Moreover, it places more responsibility for learning where it belongs – with the student.

While students work together in pairs, you can circulate among them, giving help on a more personal basis. To provide variety, the pair-work activities can be used as a listening exercise, with the teacher playing the part of Student A and the whole class playing Student B. Alternatively, one student can be Student A and the rest of the class can be Student B.

Rhythm practice: Rhythm is taught mainly through the Music of English boxes, but it is also effective when physical activity is included, such as marking time by tapping the table or moving the body in some way. The Teacher's Resource and Assessment Book suggests a variety of physical activities to reinforce the target rhythm.

Linking final sounds: Linking practice helps with listening comprehension, since words in word groups typically run together and are linked as much as possible to keep the group together. Also, this kind of practice helps students concentrate on the particular sound being studied. Linking is shown in this book by linking lines within printed words or by running words together in the gray word boxes.

Another good use for linking practice is to choose any difficult sound, such as /l/. For instance, sometimes it is difficult for learners to combine "tell" with a word that begins with a vowel, like "everybody." It should sound like "telleverybody." The reason this approach can help with a troublesome sound is that it may be easier for students to say this sound at the beginning of a word rather than at the end.

Pitch patterns: English language learners usually do not hear intonation very well. When they listen to speech, they are powerfully distracted from paying attention to pitch changes because they are struggling to understand sounds, vocabulary, and grammar. The pitch lines in the Music of English boxes remind students of the importance of pitch patterns in English.

Games: Some units include various types of games for extra practice. If class time allows, these tasks can help consolidate the material practiced in the unit.

Pyramid reviews: Some units end with review tasks in which students fill in parts of the pronunciation pyramid. These exercises can help students gradually practice noticing the key elements in a word group.

Extra practice: If your students need additional work with the vowel sounds and rules, use the exercises in Extra Practice 1, "Vowels," at the end of the book. If your students need more practice with some common problem consonant sounds, use the exercises in Extra Practice 2, "Problem consonants."

Use as many visual, kinesthetic, and auditory tools with these tasks as you can think of. There are imaginative tips from teachers included in the Teacher's Resource and Assessment Book.

Components of *Clear Speech From the Start,* Second Edition

In addition to this Student's Book, this second edition of *Clear Speech From the Start* also includes the following components:

- **Teacher's Resource and Assessment Book** with practical explanations for the rationale for each lesson, useful classroom procedures, teaching tips, as well as the audio script and answer key for each task. It also includes a listening diagnostic test, a speaking diagnostic test and a student pronunciation profile form, 15 unit quizzes, and all the audio scripts and answer keys.

- **Class Audio and Assessment CDs** with three CDs including the audio for all the listening tasks in the Student's Book and one CD including the audio for all the tasks in the listening test and quizzes.

- **App** *Basic Pronunciation: Clear Speech From the Start* for iPhone, iPad, and iPod touch, with hundreds of fun interactive activities for engaging practice with word stress, syllables, and beginning and final sounds. It is available on the App Store.

- **Website** (www.cambridge.org/clearspeech) with extra materials and information about the series, including the complete audio for all the listening activities in the Student's Book as downloadable MP3s.

Key to Sound Symbols

VOWELS			
Key words	*Clear Speech From the Start*	*Cambridge Dictionary of American English/ International Phonetic Alphabet*	Your dictionary
cake, mail, pay	/eʸ/	/eɪ/	
pan, bat, hand	/æ/	/æ/	
tea, feet, key	/iʸ/	/i:/	
ten, well, red	/ɛ/	/e/	
ice, pie, night	/aʸ/	/aɪ/	
is, fish, will	/ɪ/	/ɪ/	
cone, road, know	/oʷ/	/oʊ/	
top, rock, stop	/ɑ/	/ɑ/	
blue, school, new, cube, few	/uʷ/	/u:/	
cut, cup, us, rust, love	/ʌ/	/ʌ/	
house, our, cow	/aʷ/	/aʊ/	
saw, talk, applause	/ɔ/	/ɔ:/	
boy, coin, join	/ɔʸ/	/ɔɪ/	
put, book, woman	/ʊ/	/ʊ/	
alone, open, pencil, atom, ketchup	/ə/	/ə/	

CONSONANTS			
Key words	*Clear Speech From the Start*	*Cambridge Dictionary of American English/ International Phonetic Alphabet*	**Your dictionary**
bid, jo**b**	/b/	/b/	
do, fee**d**	/d/	/d/	
food, sa**f**e, lea**f**	/f/	/f/	
go, do**g**	/g/	/g/	
home, be**h**ind	/h/	/h/	
kiss, ba**ck**	/k/	/k/	
load, poo**l**, fai**l**	/l/	/l/	
man, plu**m**	/m/	/m/	
need, ope**n**	/n/	/n/	
pen, ho**p**e	/p/	/p/	
road, ca**r**d	/r/	/r/	
see, re**c**ent	/s/	/s/	
show, na**ti**on, wa**sh**	/ʃ/	/ʃ/	
team, mea**t**	/t/	/t/	
choose, wa**tch**	/tʃ/	/tʃ/	
think, bo**th**, tee**th**	/θ/	/θ/	
this, fa**th**er, tee**th**e	/ð/	/ð/	
visit, sa**v**e, lea**v**e	/v/	/v/	
watch, awa**y**	/w/	/w/	
yes, on**i**on	/y/	/j/	
zoo, the**s**e, ea**s**e	/z/	/z/	
bei**g**e, mea**s**ure, A**s**ia	/ʒ/	/ʒ/	
jump, bri**dg**e	/dʒ/	/dʒ/	

For interview:

Name

contry of orijin

longuages spoken

what do you do for a living?

what is your occupation?

Clear
Speech
From the Start

How Ya doing?
How are YOU doing?

Formal
How do YOU do?
It's a Pleasure to meet YOU

what's UP?
what is haPPening?

How is it going?
   How'Zit

Nice to meet YOU
   ~ ~ meecha

what is UP?
   SUP

The Alphabet and Vowels

Cake, please.

 A **The alphabet**

Listen.

Aa	Bb	Cc	Dd	Ee	Ff	Gg	Hh	Ii	Jj	Kk	Ll	Mm
Nn	Oo	Pp	Qq	Rr	Ss	Tt	Uu	Vv	Ww	Xx	Yy	Zz

 B **Vowel letters**

Listen.

a　　e　　i　　o　　u

 C **Do you hear *a*?**

1 Listen. Mark Yes or No.

	Yes	**No**	
1.	✔	....	(cake)
2.	....	✔	(rice)
3.	✓	....	Pu*y*
4.	....	✓	so
5.	....	✓	seat
6.	✓	....	make

a

cake

2 Listen again.

 D **Do you hear *e*?**

1 Listen. Mark Yes or No.

	Yes	**No**	
1.	✔	....	(tea)
2.	....	✓	ten
3.	....	✓	toe
4.	✓	....	cheess
5.	....	....	
6.	✓	....	Please

e

tea

2 Listen again.

E Do you hear *i*?

1 Listen. Mark Yes or No.

	Yes	No	
1.	✓		ice
2.	✓		tie
3.		✓	soy
4.	✓		Hi
5.	✓		fries
6.		✓	cheess

i

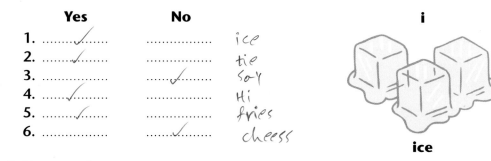

ice

2 Listen again.

F Do you hear *o*?

1 Listen. Mark Yes or No.

	Yes	No	
1.	✓		cone
2.	✓		so
3.	✓		go
4.		✓	cone
5.	✓		Boot
6.		✓	fries

o

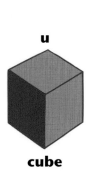

cone

2 Listen again.

G Do you hear *u*?

1 Listen. Mark Yes or No.

	Yes	No	
1.	✓		cUbe
2.		✓	me
3.	✓		cUte
4.	✓		Use
5.		✓	cone
6.	✓		Juice

u

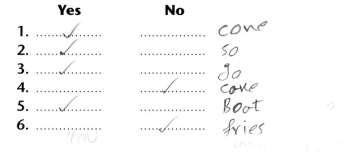

cube

2 Listen again.

H # Which word is different?

1 Listen to three words. One word is different. Mark it.

	X	Y	Z	
1.	....	....	.... ✔	(see, see, say)
2.	....	....	......✓......	tea – tea – tie
3.	....	......✓......	....	me – my – me
4.	....	...✓......	....	
5.	....	...✓......	....	Place – Please – Place
6.	....	....	......✓......	so – so – say
7.	....	....	....	two – toe – t
8.	....	......✓......	....	why – we – why

2 Listen again.

I # Saying the alphabet vowel sounds

Listen. Then say each sound until you can say it easily.

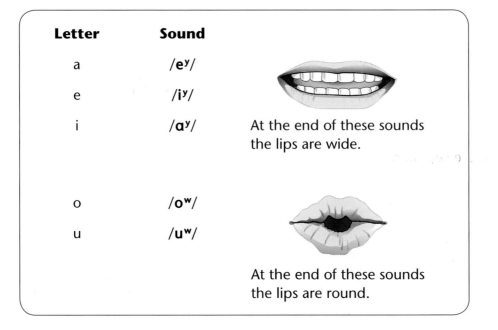

Letter	Sound
a	/e^y/
e	/i^y/
i	/a^y/

At the end of these sounds the lips are wide.

Letter	Sound
o	/o^w/
u	/u^w/

At the end of these sounds the lips are round.

⌢J Key words for the alphabet vowel sounds

1 Listen. Then say each key word until you can say it easily.

Letter	Sound	Key word	
a	/e^y/	cake	
e	/i^y/	tea	
i	/a^y/	ice	
o	/o^w/	cone	
u	/u^w/	cube	

2 Write the key words.

Letter	Key word
a	cake
e	tea
i	ice
o	cone
u	cube

K **Food**

Listen. Say each word until you can say it easily.

Fast Burger

MEALS

FastBurger
Cheeseburger
French fries

DESSERTS

Ice cream cones
• vanilla
• chocolate
Pie
Cake
Fruit

BEVERAGES

Juice
Lemonade
Coffee
Tea
Milk
Shakes
• vanilla
• chocolate

L **Music of English**

Listen. Then repeat each sentence until you can say it easily. Learn it like a little song.

Cake, please.

Tea, please.

2 The Two Vowel Rule

How do you spell "time"?

🎧 A Saying the letters of the alphabet

1 Listen. Then say the alphabet vowel sounds and key words.

Letter	Sound	Key word	
a	/e^y/	cake	
e	/i^y/	tea	
i	/a^y/	ice	
o	/o^w/	cone	
u	/u^w/	cube	

2 Listen. Then say the names of the alphabet letters. Notice the alphabet vowel sounds in the names of the letters.

a b c d e f g h i j k l m
n o p q r s t u v w x y z

🎧 B The Two Vowel Rule

1 Listen. Then say each word until you can say it easily.

2 Underline the first vowel letter in each word.

1. m<u>a</u>ke
2. r<u>i</u>ce
3. t<u>e</u>a
4. p<u>i</u>e
5. h<u>o</u>me
6. c<u>u</u>be
7. s<u>o</u>ap
8. <u>u</u>se

3 Read this rule.

> ### The Two Vowel Rule*
>
> When there are two vowel letters in a short word:
>
> **1.** The first vowel letter says its alphabet name.
>
> **2.** The second vowel letter is silent.
>
> This rule is true for many words.
>
> cake   tea   ice   cone   cube

🎧 C Words that end in the vowel letter -*e*-

Listen. Then say each word until you can say it easily.

/eʸ/	/iʸ/	/aʸ/	/oʷ/	/uʷ/
cake	Pete	ice	note	use
bake	see	rice	cone	cube
make	three	time	those	June
came	these	nine	home	rule
same	please	like	nose	cute

NOTE: Some words with the letter -**u**-, like "use," "cube," and "cute," have a /y/ sound before the /uʷ/ sound. But a simple /uʷ/, as in words like "June" and "rule," is more common.

* For more information on vowel rules, check Appendices B and C on pages 130–133.

D Words with two vowel letters together

Listen. Then say each word until you can say it easily.

/eʸ/	/iʸ/	/aʸ/	/oʷ/	/uʷ/
rain	eat	pie	boat	cue
train	meat	tie	Joe	suit
paid	read	fries	soap	fruit
wait	see	cries	coat	blue

E Which vowel letter says its name?

1 For each word, underline the vowel letter that says its name.

1. m<u>a</u>de	paid	name	change	cake	Jane	Jake
2. cream	please	see	cheese	three	Pete	meet
3. time	size	rice	like	write	bike	Mike
4. soak	cone	boat	smoke	Joe	bone	home
5. cute	cube	true	fruit	Sue	due	mule

2 Check your answers with the class.

F Which vowel sound is it?

1 Listen. Then say each word until you can say it easily.

meat	meal	came	made	tune	soap
close	cue	like	cheese	mile	rain

2 Write each word above in the correct box below.

/eʸ/ **cake**	/iʸ/ **tea**	/aʸ/ **ice**	/oʷ/ **cone**	/uʷ/ **cube**
came	meat			

3 Listen again and check your answers.

G Music of English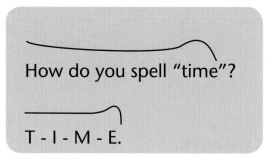

Listen. Then repeat each sentence until you can say it easily. Learn it like a little song.

How do you spell "time"?

T - I - M - E.

H Pair work: Asking how to spell words

1 Listen.

2 Say the conversations with a partner.

Student A: How do you spell "same"?
Student B: S - A - M - E.
Student A: Right.

Student B: How do you spell "cone"?
Student A: C - A - N - E.
Student B: No, it's C - O - N - E.

I Pair work: How do you spell "cheese"?

Student A: Ask how to spell a word from the Words box on the next page.
Student B: Spell the word.

Take turns asking the questions.

Examples

Student A: How do you spell "cheese"?
Student B: C - H - E - E - S - E.
Student A: Right.

Student B: How do you spell "tree"?
Student A: T - E - A.
Student B: No, it's T - R - E - E.

Words

sale	same	take	cake	page
tea	tree	cheese	please	each
ice	size	rice	time	fries
close	hope	cone	coat	soap
cute	use	cube	fruit	suit

 J **Spelling game** EXTRA

1 Divide into Team A and Team B.

2 Team A student: Say the number and letter of a word from the box below.
Team B student: Spell and pronounce the word.

3 Teams take turns asking the questions.
Teams get one point for each correct answer.

Examples

Team A student: E-4

Team B student: S - H - A - K - E. Shake.

Team B student: B-3

Team A student: P - E - T - E. Pete.

	1	2	3	4	5
A	made	name	Mike	Jane	pie
B	please	sale	Pete	team	page
C	cute	cheese	June	write	each
D	change	ice	boat	time	fries
E	cake	rice	cone	shake	soap

3 | Syllables

How many syllables are in "city"?

🎧 A Syllables ☐ ☐ ☐

1 A syllable is a small part of a word. Listen.

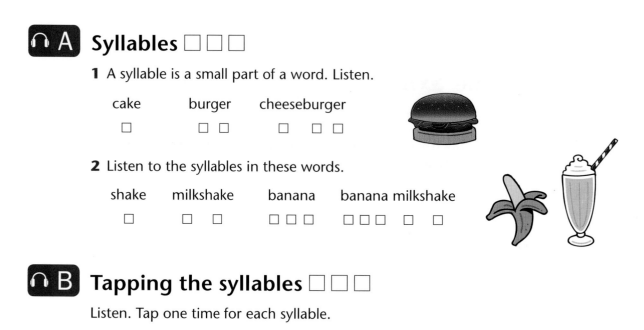

cake	burger	cheeseburger
☐	☐ ☐	☐ ☐ ☐

2 Listen to the syllables in these words.

shake	milkshake	banana	banana milkshake
☐	☐ ☐	☐ ☐ ☐	☐ ☐ ☐ ☐ ☐

🎧 B Tapping the syllables ☐ ☐ ☐

Listen. Tap one time for each syllable.

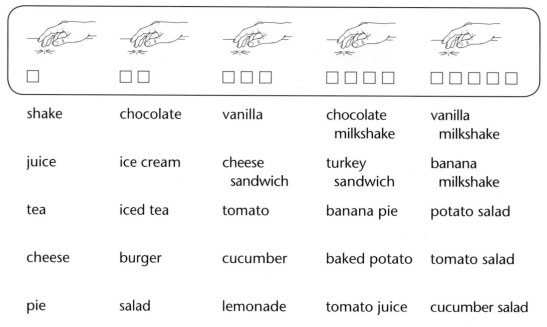

☐	☐ ☐	☐ ☐ ☐	☐ ☐ ☐ ☐	☐ ☐ ☐ ☐ ☐
shake	chocolate	vanilla	chocolate milkshake	vanilla milkshake
juice	ice cream	cheese sandwich	turkey sandwich	banana milkshake
tea	iced tea	tomato	banana pie	potato salad
cheese	burger	cucumber	baked potato	tomato salad
pie	salad	lemonade	tomato juice	cucumber salad

C Counting syllables ☐ ☐ ☐

1 Listen. Write the number of syllables you hear.

1. ......2...... (cola)
2. ....
3. ....
4. ....
5. ....
6. ....
7. ....
8. ....
9. ....
10. ....

2 Listen again. Did you write the correct number?

⌒ D Which word is different?

1 Listen to three words. One word is different. Mark it.

	X	Y	Z	
1.	....	....	✔	(sit, sit, city)
2.	....	....	....	
3.	....	....	....	
4.	....	....	....	
5.	....	....	....	
6.	....	....	....	
7.	....	....	....	
8.	....	....	....	
9.	....	....	....	
10.	....	....	....	

2 Listen again. Did you mark the correct answer?

E Pair work: One or two syllables? ☐☐☐

Student A: Say word **a** or word **b**.

Student B: Hold up one or two fingers.

Take turns saying the words below.

Examples

Student A: Ninety.

Student B: (Hold up two fingers.)

Student B: Eight.

Student A: (Hold up one finger.)

1. a. ninety
   b. nine

2. a. eighty
   b. eight

3. a. four
   b. forty

4. a. sixty
   b. six

5. a. rain
   b. raining

6. a. rented
   b. rent

7. a. store
   b. a store

8. a. sit
   b. city

9. a. blow
   b. below

10. a. cleaned
    b. clean it

🎧 F Tapping syllables in words ☐☐☐

1 Listen.

2 Cover the words. Listen again. Say each word and tap the syllables.

3 Write the number of syllables.

1. banana   1. ......*3*......
2. sandwich   2. ....
3. milkshake   3. ....
4. painted   4. ....
5. rented   5. ....
6. closed   6. ....
7. opened   7. ....
8. cleaned   8. ....

G Tapping syllables in groups of words ☐☐☐

Listen. Say each group of words and tap the syllables.

1. a cheeseburger
2. a vanilla milkshake

3. pie or ice cream
4. two salads and one milk

H Music of English 🎵

Listen. Then repeat each sentence until you can say it easily. Learn it like a little song.

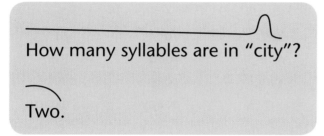

How many syllables are in "city"?

Two.

I Pair work: How many syllables are in "forty"? ☐☐☐

Student A: Choose a word from the Words box. Ask how many syllables are in the word.

Student B: Hold up one, two, or three fingers.

Take turns asking the questions.

Examples

Student A: How many syllables are in "forty"?
Student B: (Hold up two fingers.)

Student B: How many syllables are in "vanilla"?
Student A: (Hold up three fingers.)

Words

city	salad	burger	class	vanilla
forty	computer	coffee	milkshake	cucumber

J The Two Vowel Rule for syllables

1 Read the rule.

> ### The Two Vowel Rule*
>
> When there are two vowel letters in a syllable:
>
> **1.** The first vowel letter says its alphabet name.
>
> **2.** The second vowel letter is silent.
>
> This rule is true for many words.
>
> | | | | | |
> |---|---|---|---|---|
> | cake | tea | ice | cone | cube |
> | remain | repeat | arrive | soapy | fruit |

2 Listen. Then say each word until you can say it easily.

/eʸ/	/iʸ/	/aʸ/	/oʷ/	/uʷ/
rain	please	wife	road	true
explain	repeat	mine	soap	juice
bake	complete	arrive	soapy	excuse

K Music of English

Listen. Then repeat each sentence until you can say it easily. Learn it like a little song.

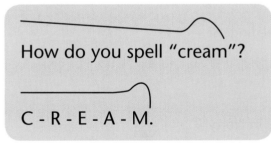

How do you spell "cream"?

C - R - E - A - M.

---

* For more information on the vowel rules, check Appendices B and C on pages 130–133.

L Pair work: How do you spell "city"?

Student A: Ask question **a** or question **b**.
Student B: Answer.

Take turns asking the questions.

Examples

Student A: How do you spell "sit"?
Student B: S - I - T.

Student B: How do you spell "forty"?
Student A: F - O - U - R.
Student B: No, it's F - O - R - T - Y.

1. a. How do you spell "city"?   C - I - T - Y.
   b. How do you spell "sit"?   S - I - T.

2. a. How do you spell "store"?   S - T - O - R - E.
   b. How do you spell "a store"?   A S - T - O - R - E.

3. a. How do you spell "four"?   F - O - U - R.
   b. How do you spell "forty"?   F - O - R - T - Y.

4. a. How do you spell "rent"?   R - E - N - T.
   b. How do you spell "rented"?   R - E - N - T - E - D.

5. a. How do you spell "raining"?   R - A - I - N - I - N - G.
   b. How do you spell "rain"?   R - A - I - N.

6. a. How do you spell "soap"?   S - O - A - P.
   b. How do you spell "soapy"?   S - O - A - P - Y.

7. a. How do you spell "seventy"?   S - E - V - E - N - T - Y.
   b. How do you spell "seven"?   S - E - V - E - N.

8. a. How do you spell "salt"?   S - A - L - T.
   b. How do you spell "salad"?   S - A - L - A - D.

M Food game EXTRA

1 Divide into teams.

2 Each team thinks of food words and writes the words in the boxes.

3 After five minutes, compare your boxes. Each team gets one point for each syllable.

1 syllable ☐	2 syllables ☐☐	3 syllables ☐☐☐	4 syllables ☐☐☐☐
rice	ice cream	banana	macaroni

N Review: The Two Vowel Rule

Notice the vowel sounds in these words.

/eʸ/   /iʸ/   /aʸ/   /oʷ/   /uʷ/

cake   tea   ice   cone   cube

4 The One Vowel Rule
Linking with /n/

What does "less" mean?
How do you say S - H - A - K - E?

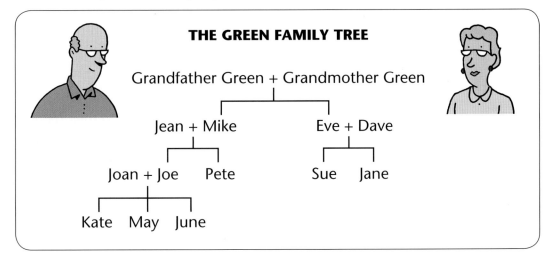 A The Green family and the Two Vowel Rule

1 This is a family tree. These people are all relatives. Listen to their names.

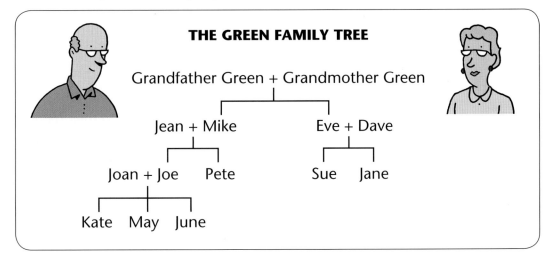

THE GREEN FAMILY TREE

Grandfather Green + Grandmother Green

Jean + Mike   Eve + Dave

Joan + Joe   Pete   Sue   Jane

Kate   May   June

2 In the Green family, all the names follow the Two Vowel Rule. Review the rule.

The Two Vowel Rule

When there are two vowel letters in a syllable:

1. The first vowel letter says its **alphabet** name.

2. The second vowel letter is silent.

This rule is true for many words.

remain	repeat	arrive	soapy	excuse
Jane	Jean	Mike	Joe	Sue

B Pair work: Questions about the Green family

Ask your partner questions about the Green family. Write your answers.

1. Who is Joe's brother? .... Pete ....
2. Who is Jane's sister? ....
3. Who is Eve's mother? ....
4. Who is May's father? ....
5. Who is Grandmother Green's son? ....
6. Who are Kate's sisters? ....
7. Who is Dave's wife? ....
8. Who are Jean's sons? ....

∩ C The Red family and the One Vowel Rule

1 This is the Red family. These people are all relatives. Listen to their names.

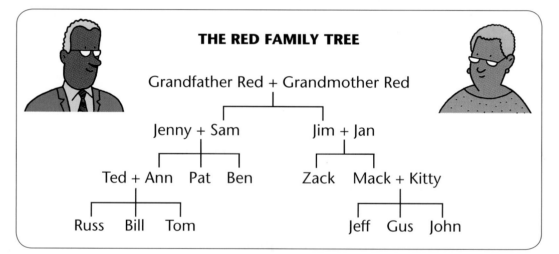

THE RED FAMILY TREE

Grandfather Red + Grandmother Red

Jenny + Sam   Jim + Jan

Ted + Ann   Pat   Ben   Zack   Mack + Kitty

Russ   Bill   Tom   Jeff   Gus   John

2 In the Red family, all the names follow the One Vowel Rule.

The One Vowel Rule

When there is only one vowel letter in a syllable:

1. The vowel letter says its **relative** sound.

2. This sound is a relative of the alphabet vowel, but it is not the same sound.

This rule is true for many words.

can	pencil	finger	hot	summer
Mack	Jenny	Kitty	John	Russ

D Words with relative vowel sounds

Listen.

/æ/	/ɛ/	/ɪ/	/ɑ/	/ʌ/
cat	red	is	on	bus
hat	bed	his	hot	mud
apple	pen	sister	pot	sun
thanks	sell	finish	block	uncle
happy	rest	little	sock	supper

E Key words for the relative vowel sounds

1 Listen. Then say each key word until you can say it easily.

Vowel letter	Relative sound	Key word	
a	/æ/	man	
e	/ɛ/	men	
i	/ɪ/	pill	
o	/ɑ/	pot	
u	/ʌ/	sun	

2 Write the key words for the relative vowel sounds.

Vowel letter	Relative sound key word
a	....
e	....
i	....
o	....
u	....

⌢ F The difference between alphabet vowel sounds and relative vowel sounds

Remember, alphabet vowel sounds say their alphabet names.
Relative vowel sounds are different.

1 Listen. These names have alphabet vowel sounds.

/eʸ/	/iʸ/	/aʸ/	/oʷ/	/uʷ/
Jane	Jean	Mike	Joe	June

2 Listen. These names have relative vowel sounds.

/æ/	/ɛ/	/ɪ/	/ɑ/	/ʌ/
Jan	Jen	Bill	Tom	Gus

⌢ G Do you hear /æ/?

1 Listen. Mark Yes or No.

/æ/

	Yes	No	
1.	✔	....	(man)
2.	....	✔	(main)
3.	....	....	
4.	....	....	
5.	....	....	
6.	....	....	

man

2 Listen again.

⌢ H Do you hear /ɛ/?

1 Listen. Mark Yes or No.

/ɛ/

	Yes	No	
1.	✔	....	(men)
2.	....	....	
3.	....	....	
4.	....	....	
5.	....	....	
6.	....	....	

men

2 Listen again.

I Do you hear /ɪ/?

1. Listen. Mark Yes or No.

	Yes	No
1.	....	....
2.	....	....
3.	....	....
4.	....	....
5.	....	....
6.	....	....

/ɪ/

pill

2 Listen again.

J Do you hear /ɑ/?

1 Listen. Mark Yes or No.

	Yes	No
1.	....	....
2.	....	....
3.	....	....
4.	....	....
5.	....	....
6.	....	....

/ɑ/

pot

2 Listen again.

K Do you hear /ʌ/?

1 Listen. Mark Yes or No.

	Yes	No
1.	....	....
2.	....	....
3.	....	....
4.	....	....
5.	....	....
6.	....	....

/ʌ/

sun

2 Listen again.

L Which word is different?

1 Listen to three words. One word is different. Mark it.

	X	Y	Z	
1.	....	........✔........	....	(mate, mat, mate)
2.	....	....	....	
3.	....	....	....	
4.	....	....	....	
5.	....	....	....	
6.	....	....	....	
7.	....	....	....	

2 Listen again.

M Listening to vowel sounds

Listen. Point to each word as you hear it.

/eʸ/	/æ/	/iʸ/	/ɛ/	/aʸ/	/ɪ/	/oʷ/	/ɑ/	/uʷ/	/ʌ/
Kate	cat	teen	ten	ice	is	load	lot	cute	cut
Jane	Jan	Jean	Jen	file	fill	Joan	John	cube	cub
ate	at	meat	met	time	Tim	hope	hop	rule	run
same	Sam	seat	set	bite	bit	coat	cot	tube	tub

 ## N Which vowel sound do you hear?

1 Listen. Some words have alphabet vowel sounds and some have relative vowel sounds.

cute	teen	rule	ride	pine	lease
made	road	main	cube	ice	coast
hop	shake	less	mad	rod	man
cheese	fun	chess	cub	shack	ten
rid	cut	hot	is	hope	pin

2 Write the words in the correct boxes. Each box has three words.

/eʸ/	/iʸ/	/aʸ/	/oʷ/	/uʷ/
made	cheese			cute

/æ/	/ɛ/	/ɪ/	/ɑ/	/ʌ/
		rid	hop	

3 Check your answers with the class.

🎧 0 ## Music of English ♪

Listen. Then repeat each sentence until you can say it easily.

What does "less" mean?

What does "lease" mean?

How do you say S - H - A - K - E?

P Pair work: How do you say S - H - A - K - E?

Student A: Ask question **a** or question **b**.

Student B: Answer the question.

Take turns asking the questions.

Examples

Student A: What does "less" mean?

Student B: Not as much.

Student B: How do you say S - H - A - K - E?

Student A: Shake.

1. a. What does "lease" mean?   To rent, usually for a year.
   b. What does "less" mean?   Not as much.

2. a. How do you say
      S - H - A - C - K?   Shack.
   b. How do you say
      S - H - A - K - E?   Shake.

3. a. What does "shake" mean?   A drink made of ice cream.
   b. What does "shack" mean?   A very poor house.

4. a. How do you say
      L - E - A - S - E?   Lease.
   b. How do you say
      L - E - S - S?   Less.

5. a. How do you say I - C - E?   Ice.
   b. How do you say I - S?   Is.

6. a. What does "main" mean?   The most important.
   b. What does "man" mean?   A male person.

7. a. How do you say
      C - H - E - S - S?   Chess.
   b. How do you say
      C - H - E - E - S - E?   Cheese.

8. a. What does "made" mean?   The past of "make."
   b. What does "mad" mean?   Angry.

Q Linking with /n/ ⌘

Many words are linked together.

1 The sound **/n/** links to a vowel sound at the beginning of the next word. Listen.

Dan is. Dannis .

an apple annnapple

2 The sound **/n/** links to another **/n/** sound at the beginning of the next word. Listen.

John knows. Johnnnknows .

ten names tennnnames

R More linking with /n/ ⌘

Listen. Then say each sentence until you can say it easily. Remember to link **/n/** to the sound at the beginning of the next word.

1. Dan is here.   Dannis here.

2. Ken asks questions.   Kennnasks questions.

3. Jan and I will go.   Jannnand I will go.

4. Joan always goes.   Joannnalways goes.

5. Jean never goes.   Jeannnnever goes.

6. John knows everything. Johnnnknows everything.

7. This is an ice cube.   This is annnice cube.

8. I want an apple.   I want annnapple .

9. The list has ten names. The list has tennnnames .

10. Have you seen Nancy?   Have you seennnNancy ?

S Game: What vowel sound does the letter have? EXTRA

1 Divide into small teams.

2 Say the names of the alphabet letters. Notice how each letter is pronounced with a vowel sound.

a b c d e f g h i j k l m n o p q r s t u v w x y z

3 Put the letters of the alphabet under the correct vowel sounds in the chart.

4 Check your answers with the other teams.

NOTE: The letter -**r**- does not belong in any of these groups. It is pronounced like the word "are."

/eʸ/ cake	/iʸ/ tea	/ɛ/ ten	/aʸ/ ice	/oʷ/ cone	/uʷ/ cube
a	b	f			

T Review: The One Vowel Rule

Write these names under the correct vowel sound in the pyramids.

Tom Gus Jen Jan Bill

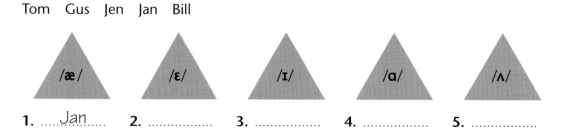

/æ/   /ɛ/   /ɪ/   /ɑ/   /ʌ/

1. Jan   2. ....   3. ....   4. ....   5. ....

5 | Strong Syllables
Linking with /m/

What's that called?
What's it for?

 A Strong syllables

1 Listen.

1. Canada
   Ca**a**nada   /æ/

2. America
   Am**e**rica   /ɛ/

3. Toronto
   Tor**o**nto   /ɑ/

4. San Francisco
   San Franc**i**sco   /ɪ/

2 Read this rule.

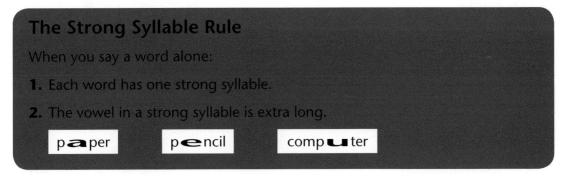

The Strong Syllable Rule

When you say a word alone:

1. Each word has one strong syllable.

2. The vowel in a strong syllable is extra long.

p**a**per   p**e**ncil   comp**u**ter

3 Listen. Then say this word until you can say it easily.

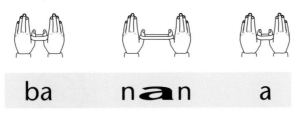

ba   n**a**n   a

🎧 B Listening for strong syllables

1 Listen for the strong syllable in each word. Underline the long vowel in the strong syllable.

1. ban<u>a</u>na
2. atomic
3. freezer
4. blanket

5. vanilla
6. chocolate
7. elephant
8. electric

2 Check your answers with the class.

🎧 C Saying strong syllables

Listen. Then say each word until you can say it easily. Make the strong vowel extra long.

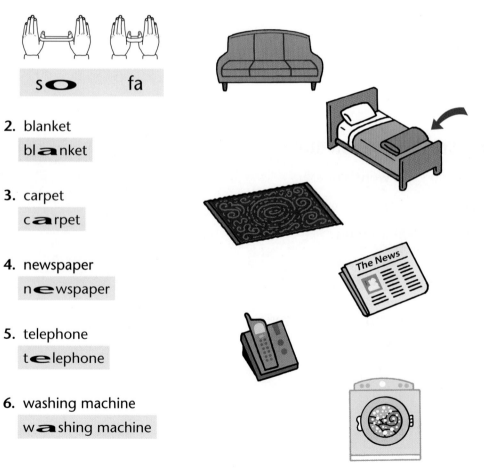

1. sofa

  s⬤   fa

2. blanket

  bl🅰nket

3. carpet

  c🅰rpet

4. newspaper

  n⬬wspaper

5. telephone

  t⬬lephone

6. washing machine

  w🅰shing machine

7. refrigerator
   refr**i**gerator

8. television
   t**e**levision

9. freezer
   fr**e**ezer

10. alarm clock
    al**a**rm clock

11. can opener
    c**a**n opener

12. vacuum cleaner
    v**a**cuum cleaner

13. ceiling
    c**e**iling

14. bathtub
    b**a**thtub

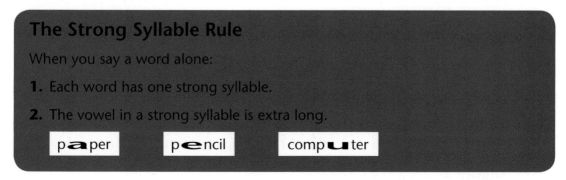

D Strong syllables in sentences

1 Review this rule.

The Strong Syllable Rule

When you say a word alone:

1. Each word has one strong syllable.

2. The vowel in a strong syllable is extra long.

p**a**per   p**e**ncil   comp**u**ter

2 Read this new rule.

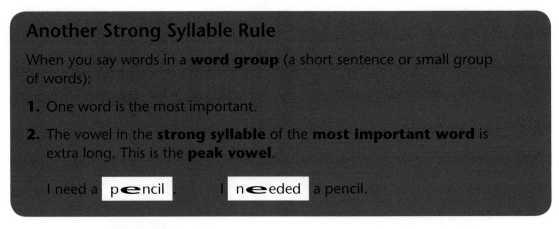

Another Strong Syllable Rule

When you say words in a **word group** (a short sentence or small group of words):

1. One word is the most important.

2. The vowel in the **strong syllable** of the **most important word** is extra long. This is the **peak vowel**.

I need a p**e**ncil.   I n**e**eded a pencil.

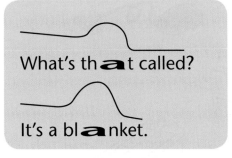

⌂ E Music of English ♪

Listen. Then repeat each sentence until you can say it easily.

What's th**a**t called?

It's a bl**a**nket.

F Pair work: What's that called?

Student A: Point to a picture on the next page and ask, "What's that called?"
Student B: Say an answer from the list below the pictures on the next page.

Take turns asking the questions.

Examples

Student A: (Point to the picture of a blanket.) What's th**a**t called?

Student B: It's a bl**a**nket .

Student B: (Point to the picture of a telephone.) What's th**a**t called?

Student A: It's a t**e**lephone .

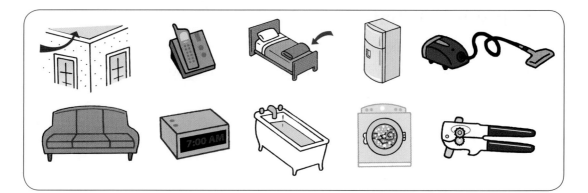

Answers

It's a telephone.	It's a can opener.
It's a sofa.	It's a blanket.
It's a washing machine.	It's an alarm clock.
It's a refrigerator.	It's a ceiling.
It's a vacuum cleaner.	It's a bathtub.

🎧 G Music of English 🎵

Listen. Then repeat each sentence until you can say it easily.

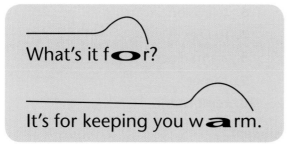

What's it f**o**r?

It's for keeping you w**a**rm.

🎧 H What's it for?

Listen. Then say each sentence until you can say it easily.

1. It's for c**a**lling people.
2. It's for keeping food c**o**ld.
3. It's for waking you **u**p.
4. It's for opening c**a**ns.
5. It's for watching sh**o**ws.

6. It's for reading the n**e**ws.
7. It's for s**i**tting on.
8. It's for cleaning the c**a**rpet.
9. It's for keeping you w**a**rm.
10. It's for washing cl**o**thes.

I Pair work: What's it for?

Student A: Say a word from the list of words below. Ask, "What's it for?"

Student B: Say an answer from the list in Task H on page 33.

Take turns asking the questions.

Examples

Student A: T**e**levision . What's it f**o**r ?

Student B: It's for watching sh**o**ws .

Student B: N**e**wspaper . What's it f**o**r ?

Student A: It's for reading the n**e**ws .

Words

television	telephone	refrigerator	newspaper	washing machine
blanket	sofa	can opener	alarm clock	vacuum cleaner

J Review: Counting syllables ☐☐☐

1 Say each word. Write the number of syllables.

1. Canada ....3.......   6. television ....
2. sofa ....   7. freezer ....
3. blanket ....   8. alarm clock ....
4. telephone ....   9. carpet ....
5. paper towels ....   10. refrigerator ....

2 Check your answers with another student.

⌒K Past -*ed* ending

1 Usually, -**ed** is added to a verb to make its past form. Listen.

Present + -ed = Past

rent	rented
need	needed
play	played
talk	talked

2 Say each word until you can say it easily. Tap the syllables.

L Extra syllable or not? ☐☐☐

Sometimes **-ed** makes an extra syllable. However, usually it does not. You will learn the syllable rule below.

1 Listen.

Present + -ed = Past

rent   rented

☐   ☐ ☐

need   needed

☐   ☐ ☐

talk   talked

☐   ☐

wash   washed

☐   ☐

plan   planned

☐   ☐

2 Listen. Hold up one finger if you hear one syllable. Hold up two fingers if you hear two syllables.

Final -t + -ed	**Final -d + -ed**	**Other final letters**
painted	added	opened
rented	loaded	walked
counted	landed	cleaned
planted	needed	closed

3 Read these rules.

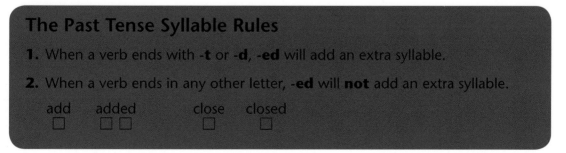

The Past Tense Syllable Rules

1. When a verb ends with **-t** or **-d**, **-ed** will add an extra syllable.

2. When a verb ends in any other letter, **-ed** will **not** add an extra syllable.

add added   close closed
☐ ☐ ☐   ☐   ☐

4 Write **-ed** after these verbs. Then say each word until you can say it easily.

Extra syllable	No extra syllable
1. want....................	8. rain....................
2. end....................	9. talk....................
3. add....................	10. wash....................
4. repeat....................	11. push....................
5. visit....................	12. look....................
6. wait....................	13. play....................
7. lift....................	14. call....................

M Pair work: Yesterday or every day?

Student A: Say sentence **a** or sentence **b**.

Student B: Say "Every day" for present or "Yesterday" for past.

Take turns saying the sentences.

Examples

Student A: We plant flowers.
Student B: Every day.

Student B: We wanted a ride.
Student A: Yesterday.

1. a. We planted flowers.
   b. We plant flowers.

2. a. We wanted a ride.
   b. We want a ride.

3. a. I need more money.
   b. I needed more money.

4. a. We painted our kitchen.
   b. We paint our kitchen.

5. a. The planes landed at the airport.
   b. The planes land at the airport.

6. a. We wait for the train.
   b. We waited for the train.

7. a. We planned meals.
   b. We plan meals.

8. a. We washed our car.
   b. We wash our car.

9. a. They looked at pictures.
   b. They look at pictures.

10. a. The children play at school.
    b. The children played at school.

🎧 N Linking with /m/ 🔗

1 The sound **/m/** links to a vowel sound at the beginning of the next word. Listen.

Jim is.　　　　　　　Jimmmis .

Come on.　　　　　　Comemmon .

2 The sound **/m/** links to another **/m/** sound at the beginning of the next word. Listen.

Tom may.　　　　　　Tommmmay .

some more　　　　　　somemmmore

3 Listen. Then say each sentence until you can say it easily.

1. Jim is here.　　　　　Jimmmis　here.

2. What time is it?　　　What　timemmis　it?

3. Sam and I will go.　　Sammmand　I will go.

4. We want some more.　We want　somemmmore .

5. Ice cream is cold.　　Ice　creammmis　cold.

6. Tom may go home.　　Tommmmay　go home.

7. Turn the alarm off.　　Turn the　alarmmmoff .

8. She came much later.　She　camemmmuch　later.

6 Weak Syllables
Linking Vowels

Can I help you?
Yes, I'd like a pizza.

A Vowels in strong and weak syllables

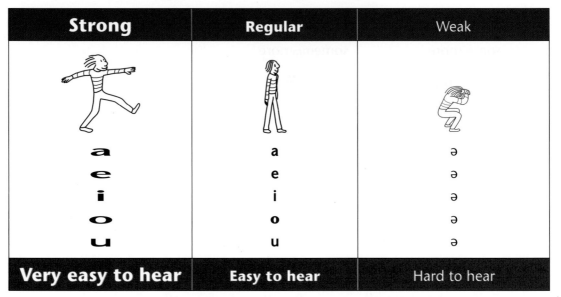

Strong	**Regular**	Weak
a e i o u	a e i o u	ə ə ə ə
Very easy to hear	**Easy to hear**	Hard to hear

B Rules for strong and weak syllables

1 Review these rules.

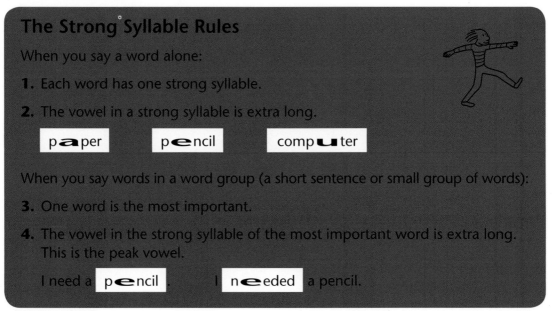

The Strong Syllable Rules

When you say a word alone:

1. Each word has one strong syllable.

2. The vowel in a strong syllable is extra long.

p**a**per   p**e**ncil   comp**u**ter

When you say words in a word group (a short sentence or small group of words):

3. One word is the most important.

4. The vowel in the strong syllable of the most important word is extra long. This is the peak vowel.

I need a p**e**ncil.   I n**e**eded a pencil.

2 Read these new rules.

The Weak Syllable Rules

1. The vowels in some syllables keep their regular sound. But some syllables get weak.

2. The vowels in weak syllables are short and not clear.

3. All weak vowels sound the same.

4. The weak vowel sound is the most common sound in spoken English.

paper	pencil	computer
papər	pencəl	cəmputər

3 Listen.

1. salad   saləd

2. lemon   lemən

3. vanilla   vənillə

4. tomato   təmato

5. lemonade   lemənade

∩ C Which vowel sounds are weak?

1 Listen. Draw a line through the weak vowels.

1. bánaná
2. Canada
3. freezer
4. blanket
5. vanilla
6. China
7. Japan

2 Check your answers with a partner.

🎧 D Saying strong and weak syllables

Listen. Then say each word until you can say it easily. Make the strong vowel extra long.

Canada
c**a**nədə

America
əm**e**rəcə

Japan
Jəp**a**n

China
Ch**i**nə

🎧 E Strong and weak syllables in food names

Listen. Then say each word until you can say it easily. Remember to make the strong vowels long and the weak vowels short.

1. salad
   s**a**ləd

2. burger
   b**u**rgər

3. celery
   c**e**ləry

4. ketchup
   k**e**tchəp

5. salmon
   s**a**lmən

6. spaghetti
   spəgh**e**tti

7. chicken
   ch**i**ckən

8. pepperoni
   peppər**o**ni

9. vanilla
   vən**i**llə

10. chocolate milk
    ch**o**colət milk

🎧 F Linking vowels ⛓️

A vowel sound at the end of a word links to a vowel sound at the beginning of the next word.

Listen. Then say each group of words until you can say it easily.

1. coffee and milk   coffeeₑand milk

2. tea and lemon   teaₑand lemon

3. pizza and salad   pizzaₐand salad

4. vanilla ice cream   vanillaₐice cream

5. banana or apple   bananaₐor apple

🎧 G Weak "and"

Usually the word "and" is so weak that it sounds like ən .
Listen. Then say each group of words until you can say it easily.

1. coffee and cream

    c**o**ffee ən cr**e**am

2. tea and lemon

    t**e**a ən l**e**mən

3. coffee and cake

    c**o**ffee ən c**a**ke

4. bread and cheese

    br**e**ad ən ch**e**ese

🎧 H Weak "and," "of," and "a"

Listen to the weak sounds of "and," "of," and "a."
Then say each group of words until you can say it easily.

1. a cup of coffee

    ə c**u**p ə c**o**ffee

2. a bowl of soup

    ə b**o**wl ə so**u**p

3. a slice of pie

    ə sl**i**ce ə p**i**e

4. a slice of lemon pie

    ə sl**i**ce ə l**e**mən p**i**e

5. a cheese sandwich with ketchup and fries

    ə ch**e**ese s**a**ndwich with k**e**tchəp ən fr**i**es

6. a salad with cheese and tomatoes

    ə s**a**ləd with ch**e**ese ən təm**a**toes

🎧 I Review: The One Vowel Rule

1 Review this rule.

> ### The One Vowel Rule
>
> When there is only one vowel letter in a syllable:
>
> **1.** The vowel letter says its relative sound.
>
> **2.** This sound is a relative of the alphabet vowel, but it is not the same sound.
>
> This rule is true for many words.
>
> | can | pencil | finger | hot | summer |
> |-----|--------|--------|-----|--------|
> | Mack | Jenny | Kitty | John | Russ |

2 Listen. Then say each word until you can say it easily.

/æ/	/ɛ/	/ɪ/	/ɑ/	/ʌ/
salad	lemon	milk	chocolate	bun
banana	egg	vanilla	bottle	butter
sandwich	ketchup	chicken	clock	mustard

🎧 J Music of English ♪

Listen. Then repeat each sentence until you can say it easily.

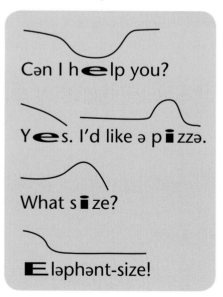

Cən I h**e**lp you?

Y**e**s. I'd like ə p**i**zzə.

What s**i**ze?

Eləphənt-size!

K The Elephant Eatery

Look at the menu. Listen. Then say each word until you can say it easily.

The Elephant Eatery

Soup (cup or bowl)
tomato soup
potato soup

Salad
green salad
carrot and raisin salad

Pizza
small   12 inches
medium   14 inches
elephant-size 16 inches

Extra toppings
extra cheese • tomatoes • pepperoni • onions • artichokes

Beverages
coffee
tea
iced tea
soda
lemonade

L Pair work: In the Elephant Eatery

1 Listen to the conversation.

2 Say the conversation with a partner.

3 Take turns as the server and the customer.

Server:	Can I help you?
Customer:	Yes, I'd like a pizza and coffee.
Server:	What kind of pizza? Plain, cheese, or with everything?
Customer:	What's everything?
Server:	Cheese, tomatoes, onions, pepperoni, and artichokes.
Customer:	Great! I want one with everything!
Server:	What size?
Customer:	Elephant-size! I'm very hungry!

Pair work: Ordering food

Order food from the Elephant Eatery menu. Take turns as the server and the customer.

Example

Server: Can I help you?

Customer: Yes, I'd like a pizza with pepperoni.

Server: What size?

Customer: Medium.

Server: OK. Anything else?

Customer: A cup of coffee, please.

Server: Coming right up!

N Food game `EXTRA`

1 Divide into teams.

2 With your team, write a list of food words with two, three, or four syllables on a piece of paper.

3 Underline the strong syllable in each word.

4 After five minutes, compare your words. Each team gets one point for each correct answer.

carrot   celery   macaroni

O Review: Strong syllables

Look at the word under each pyramid. Write the strong syllable of that word in the green level of the pyramid.

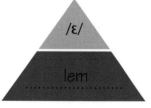

1. lemon

2. sandwich

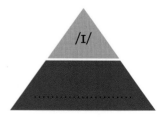

3. chicken

7 The Most Important Word

Are you going to eat dinner at nine?
No, at six.

A The most important thing

Look at these pictures. What makes the rabbit easy to see?

Hard to see

Easy to see

> **Easy to see**
>
> The rabbit is easy to see when:
> - it jumps up
> - it is extra long
> - the rabbit is light, and the leaves are dark

∩ B The most important word

1 What makes a word easy to hear?

> **Easy to hear**
>
> In English, a word is easy to hear when:
> - the strong syllable jumps up or down
> - the vowel in the strong syllable is extra long
> - the other words in the word group are weak

2 Listen.

A: What's the matter?

B: I lost a ticket.

A: What's it for?

B: It's for a show.

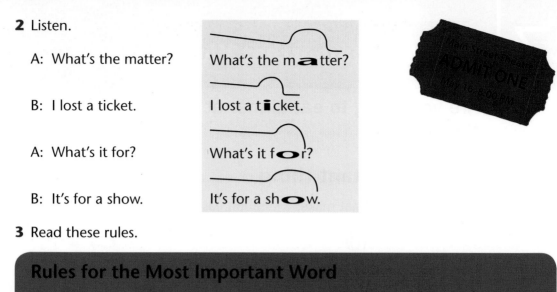

3 Read these rules.

Rules for the Most Important Word

1. Each word group (a short sentence or small group of words) has one most important word.

What's the **matter**?

2. The vowel sound in the strong syllable of that word is extra long. It is the peak vowel.

What's the m**a**tter ?

3. The voice goes up or down on the strong syllable in the most important word.

What's the m**a**tter?   What's the m**a**tter?

🎧 C Music of English 🎵

Listen. Then repeat each sentence until you can say it easily.

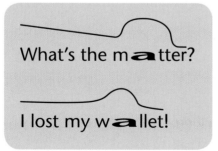

What's the m**a**tter?

I lost my w**a**llet!

D **Pair work: The most important word**

1 Listen to the conversations.

2 Say these conversations with a partner. Go up or down on the most
important word.

1. *The Glasses*

Sue: What's the m**a**tter ?   ("Matter" is the most important word.)

Ted: I lost my gl**a**sses .   ("Glasses" is the most important word.)

Sue: What k**i**nd of glasses?   ("Kind" is the most important word.)

Ted: R**e**ading glasses.   ("Reading" is the most important word.)

2. *The Keys*

Mike: What's the m**a**tter ?   ("Matter" is the most important word.)

Jane: I lost my k**e**ys .   ("Keys" is the most important word.)

Mike: Wh**i**ch keys?   ("Which" is the most important word.)

Jane: My c**a**r keys.   ("Car" is the most important word.)

E **Pair work: Finding the most important word**

1 Underline the most important word in each sentence of the conversations
on this page and on the next page.

2 Say the conversations with a partner.

1. *The Shoes*
Jean: What's <u>wrong</u>?
Joan: I lost my shoes.
Jean: Which shoes?
Joan: My tennis shoes.

2. *The Dog*

Jim: What's the problem?

Mike: I lost my dog.

Jim: What kind of dog?

Mike: A brown dog. A small brown dog.

Jim: I saw a small brown dog. It was at the supermarket.

3. *A Letter*

Bob: What are you doing?

Jenny: I'm writing a letter.

Bob: What kind of letter?

Jenny: A business letter.

Bob: What kind of business?

Jenny: Personal business!

🎧 F Music of English 🎵

Listen. Then repeat each sentence until you can say it easily.

California is a c**i**ty.

N**o**, it **i**sn't. It's a st**a**te.

Lemons are sw**e**et.

N**o**, they **a**ren't. H**o**ney is sweet.

G Pair work: Disagreement

1 Underline the most important word in each word group.

2 Say these conversations with a partner. Go up or down on the strong syllable in the important word.

1. A: California is a <u>city</u>.
   B: <u>No</u>, it <u>isn't</u>. It's a <u>state</u>.

2. A: Ice is hot.
   B: No, it isn't. It's cold.

3. A: Lemons are sweet.
   B: No, they aren't. Honey is sweet.

4. A: Babies are bigger than children.
   B: No, they aren't. They're smaller than children.

5. A: Fish eat grass.
   B: No, they don't. They eat smaller fish.

6. A: The world is flat.
   B: No, it isn't. It's round.

7. A: You buy books at a library.
   B: No, you don't. You buy books at a bookstore.

8. A: You borrow books at a bookstore.
   B: No, you don't. You borrow books at a library.

9. A: Cars travel in the air.
   B: No, they don't. They travel on the road.

10. A: Toronto is the capital of Canada.
    B: No, it isn't. Ottawa is the capital of Canada.

H Music of English ♪

Listen. Then repeat each sentence until you can say it easily.

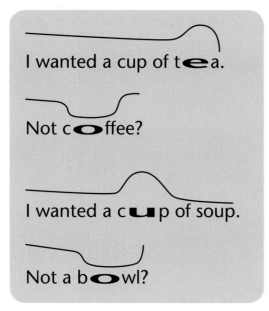

I wanted a cup of t**e**a.

Not c**o**ffee?

I wanted a c**u**p of soup.

Not a b**o**wl?

I Pair work: Misunderstandings

Customer: Say sentence **a** or sentence **b**.

Server: Answer.

Take turns as the customer and server.

NOTE: The conversations continue on the next page.

Examples

Customer: I wanted **two** lemonades.
Server: Not one?

Customer: I wanted a cup of **soup**.
Server: Not coffee?

Customer	**Server**
1. a. I wanted a cup of **soup**.	Not coffee?
b. I wanted a **cup** of soup.	Not a bowl?
2. a. I wanted **two** lemonades.	Not one?
b. I wanted two **lemonades**.	Not **lime**ades?

3. a. But I wanted lemon **pie**!   Not ice cream?
   b. But I wanted **lemon** pie!   Not apple?

4. a. I asked for potato **salad**.   Not soup?
   b. I asked for **potato** salad.   Not tomato?

5. a. This is a tuna **sandwich**!   Oh, did you want tuna salad?
   b. This is a **tuna** sandwich!   Oh, did you want egg?

6. a. That's a **small** glass!   Oh, did you want a big glass?
   b. That's a small **glass**!   Oh, did you want a cup?

🎧 J   Music of English ▲

Listen. Then repeat each sentence until you can say it easily.

Are you going to eat dinner at n**i**ne?

N**o**, at s**i**x.

Are you going to get up at s**e**ven?

N**o**, at t**e**n.

K Pair work: Correcting a mistake about time

Student A: Ask a question about an activity from the list below.
Use any time of day.

Student B: Say "No" and give another time.

Take turns asking questions. Remember to go up or down on the important word.

Examples

Student A: Are you going to get up at seven?

Student B: No, at **nine**.

Student B: Are you going to meet a friend at one?

Student A: No, at **two**.

Activities

eat breakfast	get up	catch a bus
eat lunch	go to work	meet a friend
eat dinner	have a snack	go to bed

⌢ L Review: Counting syllables ☐ ☐ ☐

1 Listen. Write the number of syllables.

1. Monday   _____2_____
2. Tuesday   _____
3. Wednesday   _____
4. Thursday   _____
5. Friday   _____
6. Saturday   _____
7. Sunday   _____

2 Check your answers with a partner.

Pair work: Correcting a mistake about the day

Student A: Ask a question about an activity from the list below. Choose any day.

Student B: Say "No" and give another day.

Take turns asking the questions.

Examples

Student A: Are you going to see the doctor on Monday?

Student B: No, **Friday**.

Student B: Are you going to play soccer on Thursday?

Student A: No, **Saturday**.

Activities

see the doctor	study English
visit friends	go to class
bake a cake	shop for clothes
fly to New York	write a letter
play soccer	wash your car
buy a car	wash the dog

Days

Monday
Tuesday
Wednesday
Thursday
Friday
Saturday
Sunday

N **Review: Most important words**

Write the most important word of the second line of the dialogue in the orange level of the pyramid.

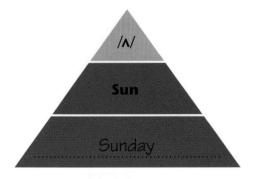

1. Are you going on Sunday?

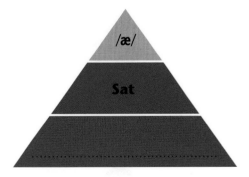

2. No, I'm going on Saturday.

8

Stop Sounds /t/ and /d/ and
Continuing Sounds /s/ and /z/
Linking with /t/, /d/, /s/, and /z/ Sounds

How do you spell "fruit"?
Is she running? No, she's reading.

🎧 A Stop sounds and continuing sounds

1 Look at these pictures.

| Stop sounds /t/ and /d/ | Continuing sounds /s/ and /z/ |

Looking to the front

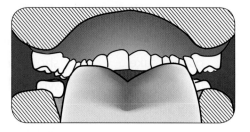

Looking down

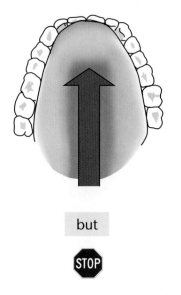
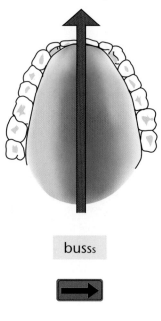

but

busss

Air stops

Air continues

2 Listen for the sound at the end of each word. Do not say the words.

	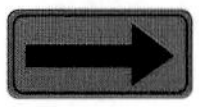
1. but	bus
but	busss
2. boat	boats
boat	boatsss
3. had	has
had	hazzz
4. seat	seats
seat	seatsss
5. it	is
it	izzz
6. hit	his
hit	hizzz

B Which word do you hear?

1 Listen. Circle the word you hear.

1. but	(bus)	(bus)
2. ticket	tickets	
3. bed	beds	
4. it	is	
5. white	wise	
6. night	nice	
7. right	rice	
8. had	has	

2 Listen again.

C Which word is different?

1 Listen to three words. One word is different. Mark it.

	X	Y	Z	
1.	....	....	......✔........	(right, right, rice)
2.	....	....	....	
3.	....	....	....	
4.	....	....	....	
5.	....	....	....	
6.	....	....	....	
7.	....	....	....	
8.	....	....	....	

2 Listen again.

⌒ D Final sounds: Stop or continue?

1 Cover the words. Listen to each word. Mark if the final sound stops or continues.

		STOP	➡
1. bus	**1.**	....	......✔........
2. but	**2.**	......✔........	....
3. rice	**3.**	....	....
4. seats	**4.**	....	....
5. had	**5.**	....	....
6. boat	**6.**	....	....
7. cheese	**7.**	....	....
8. ride	**8.**	....	....
9. cakes	**9.**	....	....
10. night	**10.**	....	....

2 Look at the words. Listen again.

E Pair work: Is it one or more than one?

Student A: Say word **a** or word **b**.

Student B: If you hear a word meaning there is one thing, hold up one finger.
If you hear a word meaning there is more than one thing, hold up
all five fingers.

Examples

Student A: Carrots.

Student B: (Hold up all five fingers.)

Student B: Jacket.

Student A: (Hold up one finger.)

1. a. carrot
    b. carrots

2. a. jackets
    b. jacket

3. a. fruit
    b. fruits

4. a. postcard
    b. postcards

5. a. coats
    b. coat

6. a. lemonade
    b. lemonades

7. a. ticket
    b. tickets

8. a. shake
    b. shakes

9. a. apple
    b. apples

10. a. seat
     b. seats

🎧 F Music of English

Listen. Then repeat each sentence until you can say it easily.

How do you spell "fr **⤿** it"?

How do you spell "rep **⤾** ats"?

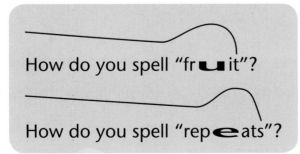

G Pair work: How do you spell "hats"?

Student A: Ask question **a** or question **b**.
Student B: Spell the word.
Student A: If the spelling is correct, say "Right." If it is wrong, say the word again.

Take turns asking the questions.

Examples

Student A: How do you spell "hats"?
Student B: H - A - T - S.
Student A: Right.

Student B: How do you spell "beds"?
Student A: B - E - D.
Student B: No, "beds."
Student A: B - E - D - S.

1. a. How do you spell "hat"?   H - A - T.
    b. How do you spell "hats"?   H - A - T - S.

2. a. How do you spell "beds"?   B - E - D - S.
    b. How do you spell "bed"?   B - E - D.

3. a. How do you spell "fruit"?   F - R - U - I - T.
    b. How do you spell "fruits"?   F - R - U - I - T - S.

4. a. How do you spell "white"?   W - H - I - T - E.
    b. How do you spell "wise"?   W - I - S - E.

5. a. How do you spell "suit"?   S - U - I - T.
    b. How do you spell "suits"?   S - U - I - T - S.

6. a. How do you spell "plate"?   P - L - A - T - E.
    b. How do you spell "plays"?   P - L - A - Y - S.

7. a. How do you spell "right"?   R - I - G - H - T.
    b. How do you spell "rice"?   R - I - C - E.

8. a. How do you spell "repeat"?   R - E - P - E - A -T.
    b. How do you spell "repeats"?   R - E - P - E - A - T - S.

H Linking with /t/ and /d/

The sounds **/t/** and **/d/** are stop sounds. At the end of a word, they link to a vowel at the beginning of the next word.

1 Listen.

bad apples   badapples

Great idea!   Greatidea !

Find it.   Findit .

2 Listen. Then say each sentence until you can say it easily.

1. These are bad apples.   These are badapples .

2. That's a great idea.   That's a greatidea .

3. Please find it.   Please findit .

4. This food is hot.   This foodis hot.

5. They counted all the money.   They countedall the money.

6. That blanket is clean.   That blanketis clean.

7. We tried every key.   We triedevery key.

8. That cat eats cheese.   That cateats cheese.

I Linking with /s/ and /z/

The sounds **/s/** and **/z/** are continuing sounds. They link to a vowel sound at the beginning of the next word. They also link to other continuing sounds.

1 Listen.

Ann's address   Annzzzaddress

Gus said.   Gussssaid .

This is Ann.   ThisssizzzAnn .

2 Listen. Then say each sentence until you can say it easily.

1. They ordered cakes and coffee. They ordered cakesₛₛand coffee.

2. Gus said, "Hello!" Gusₛₛₛsaid , "Hello!"

3. The books are on the shelf. The booksₛₛare on the shelf.

4. Put the plates on the table. Put the platesₛₛon the table.

5. It's so big! Itsₛₛₛso big!

6. Ann's address is new. Annzₐₐddressₛₛizₐₐnew .

7. She's never here. Shezₐₐnever here.

8. His mother's always late. Hizₐₐmotherzₐₐalways late.

⌒ J Review: The Two Vowel Rule

> ### The Two Vowel Rule
>
> When there are two vowel letters in a syllable:
>
> **1.** The first vowel letter says its alphabet name.
>
> **2.** The second vowel letter is silent.
>
> cake   tea   ice   cone   cube

1 These words have two vowel letters together. Listen and repeat each word.

/eʸ/	/iʸ/	/aʸ/	/oʷ/	/uʷ/
paid	need	fries	boat	blue
train	easy	tried	soak	fruit
explain	freezer	pies	coach	true
remain	reason	applied	toe	cue
complain	reading	replied	loan	suitcase

2 These words have a silent letter **-e** at the end. Listen and repeat each word.

/eʸ/	/iʸ/	/aʸ/	/oʷ/	/uʷ/
plane	these	price	note	cute
change	complete	retire	clothes	reduce
arrange	extreme	arrive	those	excuse
erase	Chinese	advice	telephone	refuse

K Music of English 🎵

Listen. Then repeat each sentence until you can say it easily.

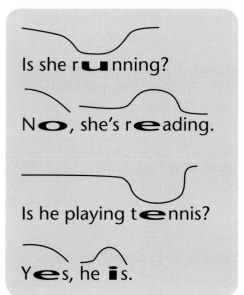

Is she r**u**nning?

N**o**, she's r**e**ading.

Is he playing t**e**nnis?

Y**e**s, he **i**s.

 L Pair work: Correcting a mistake

1 Listen. Then say the name of each activity until you can say it easily.

running	reading	drinking water	playing soccer
sleeping	eating	playing tennis	playing basketball

2 Student A: Point to a picture of an activity. Ask a question about the picture.
   Student B: Answer.

Example

Student A: Is she drinking water?
Student B: Yes, she is. (or) No, she's **eating**.

Activities

M S-Ball game EXTRA

1 Divide into groups of four or five. Each group has a small ball. One student in each group is the Leader.

2 Leader, ask a question and then throw the ball to a student in your group.

3 Student, catch the ball and answer the question. If you answer correctly (with a final **/s/** or **/z/** sound in the verb), you become the new Leader. If you don't answer correctly, return the ball to the Leader.

Example

Leader:	(Leader throws the ball to Student A.)
	What does "reader" mean?
Student A:	A person who read.
Leader:	No.
	(Student A throws the ball back to the Leader.)
	(Leader throws the ball to Student B.)
	What does "reader" mean?
Student B:	A person who reads.
Leader:	Yes.
	(Student B is now the Leader, throws the ball to a student, and asks a question.)

1. What does "baker" mean?

2. What does "worker" mean?

3. What does "reader" mean?

4. What does "cleaner" mean?

5. What does "leader" mean?

6. What does "speaker" mean?

7. What does "player" mean?

8. What does "painter" mean?

9. What does "trainer" mean?

How do you spell "whale"?
What does "paid" mean?

 A Final sounds /d/ and /l/

1 Look at these pictures.

Stop sound /d/   **Continuing sound /l/**

Looking to the front

   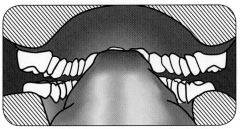

Looking down

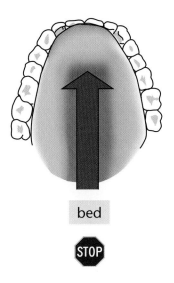   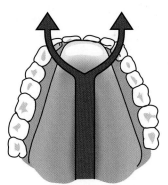

bed   bellll

Air stops   Air continues

2 Listen for the sound at the end of each word. Do not say the words.

STOP → ▶

1. food   fool
   food   foolll

2. made   mail
   made   maillll

3. road   roll
   road   rollll

4. feed   feel
   feed   feelll

5. bed   bell
   bed   bellll

🎧 B Which word do you hear?

1 Listen. Circle the word you hear.

STOP → ▶

1. (made)   mail   (made)
2. food   fool
3. road   roll
4. bed   bell
5. paid   pale
6. tide   tile
7. fade   fail
8. feed   feel

2 Listen again and check your answers.

C Which word is different?

1 Listen to three words. One word is different. Mark it.

	X	Y	Z	
1.	....	....	.......✔........	(food, food, fool)
2.	....	....	....	
3.	....	....	....	
4.	....	....	....	
5.	....	....	....	
6.	....	....	....	
7.	....	....	....	
8.	....	....	....	

2 Listen again.

D Saying final sounds /d/ and /l/

Listen. Then say each word until you can say it easily.

	🛑 STOP	➡️
1.	food	foolll
2.	made	mailll
3.	road	rollll
4.	feed	feelll
5.	bed	bellll

E Music of English 🎵

Listen. Then repeat each sentence until you can say it easily.

How do you spell "wh▲le"?

What does "p▲id" mean?

F Pair work: Hearing and saying final /d/ and /l/

Student A: Ask question **a** or question **b**.

Student B: Answer.

Student A: If the answer is correct, say "Right." If it is wrong, ask again.

Take turns asking the questions.

Examples

Student A: How do you spell "made"?

Student B: M - A - I - L.

Student A: No, "made."

Student B: M - A - D - E.

Student B: What does "fool" mean?

Student A: A silly person.

Student B: Right.

1. a. How do you spell "made"?   M - A - D - E.
   b. How do you spell "mail"?   M - A - I - L.

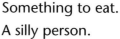

2. a. What does "food" mean?   Something to eat.
   b. What does "fool" mean?   A silly person.

3. a. How do you spell "road"?   R - O - A - D.
   b. How do you spell "roll"?   R - O - L - L.

4. a. What does "bed" mean?   A thing you sleep in.
   b. What does "bell" mean?   A thing you ring.

5. a. How do you spell "bed"?   B - E - D.
   b. How do you spell "bell"?   B - E - L - L.

6. a. What does "whale" mean?   A very big sea animal.
   b. What does "wade" mean?   To walk in water.

7. a. How do you spell "whale"?   W - H - A - L - E.
   b. How do you spell "wade"?   W - A - D - E.

8. a. What does "feed" mean?   To give food.
    b. What does "feel" mean?   To touch something.

9. a. How do you spell "feed"?   F - E - E - D.
    b. How do you spell "feel"?   F - E - E - L.

10. a. What does "paid" mean?   The past of "pay."
    b. What does "pail" mean?   A bucket.

🎧 G Listening for final /l/: Present or future?

1 Cover the sentences. Listen. Is the sentence present or future? Circle Present or Future.

2 Look at the sentences. Listen again. Were your answers correct?

1. a. I read the newspaper. b. I'll read the newspaper.	Present (Future)
2. a. I drink coffee. b. I'll drink coffee.	Present Future
3. a. I drive to work. b. I'll drive to work.	Present Future
4. a. I take the train. b. I'll take the train.	Present Future
5. a. We ride the bus. b. We'll ride the bus.	Present Future
6. a. They go home. b. They'll go home.	Present Future
7. a. We watch TV. b. We'll watch TV.	Present Future
8. a. They go to the movies. b. They'll go to the movies.	Present Future

∩ H Pair work: Present or future?

1 Listen. Then say these words until you can say them easily.

Present	Future
every day	tomorrow
every night	tonight
every week	next week

2 Student A: Say sentence **a** or sentence **b**.

Student B: Say words from the box above to complete the sentence.

Take turns saying the sentences.

Examples

Student A: We eat cake.

Student B: Every night.

Student B: We'll ask questions.

Student A: Tonight.

1. a. We eat cake.
   b. We'll eat cake.

2. a. We ask questions.
   b. We'll ask questions.

3. a. They cut the bread.
   b. They'll cut the bread.

4. a. They go to the store.
   b. They'll go to the store.

5. a. I buy fish.
   b. I'll buy fish.

6. a. I cook dinner.
   b. I'll cook dinner.

7. a. We read the newspaper.
   b. We'll read the newspaper.

8. a. We work hard.
   b. We'll work hard.

I Linking with /l/ 🔗

The sound **/l/** is a continuing sound, like **/s/**, **/z/**, **/m/**, and **/n/**. Vowels are also continuing sounds.

1 Listen. Notice how the **/l/** links to the continuing sound at the beginning of the next word.

Sell it.   Sellllit .

Tell me.   Tellllme .

2 Listen. Then say each sentence until you can say it easily.

1. Sell it now.   Sellllit now.

2. Tell us everything.   Tellllus everything.

3. Do you feel OK?   Do you feellllOK ?

4. Will you go?   Willllyou go?

5. How do you spell "whale"? How do you spellllwhale ?

6. These books are all new. These books are allllnew .

7. Tell me all you know.   Tellllme allllyou know.

8. Tom will look for the key. Tom willlllook for the key.

J Review: Counting syllables in sentences ▢▢▢

1 Cover the sentences. Listen. Then say each sentence until you can say it easily.

2 Write the number of syllables in each sentence.

1. Make a bowl of rice.   1. ......5......
2. We need two plates.   2. ....
3. They like ice cubes.   3. ....
4. Joe needed five tickets.   4. ....
5. We cleaned the plates.   5. ....

3 Read the sentences aloud. Check your answers with a partner.

Did you say "coal"?
No, I said "cold."

A Final sounds /l/ and /ld/

Listen to the final sounds in these words.

	→	STOP
1.	call	called
2.	pull	pulled
3.	mail	mailed
4.	bowl	bold
5.	sail	sailed
6.	fill	filled
7.	coal	cold

B Present and past

1 Read the sentences.

2 Cover the sentences. Listen. Mark Present or Past.

		Present	Past	
1.	I called a friend.	1	...........✔........	(called)
2.	I sail a boat on Sundays.	2	....	
3.	We mail a letter every day.	3	....	
4.	We mailed everything.	4	....	
5.	We fill our glasses.	5	....	
6.	A cow made our milk.	6	....	
7.	We sealed all the letters.	7	....	

3 Listen again. Then say the sentences until you can say them easily. Make a clear difference between the present and past verbs.

C Pair work: What does "mail" mean?

Student A: Ask question **a** or question **b**.
Student B: Answer.

Take turns asking the questions.

Examples

Student A: What does "mail" mean?
Student B: Things like letters and postcards.

Student B: What does "pulled" mean?
Student A: The past of "pull."

1. a. What does "made" mean?   The past of "make."
   b. What does "mail" mean?   Things like letters and postcards.

2. a. What does "pull" mean?   The opposite of "push."
   b. What does "pulled" mean?   The past of "pull."

3. a. What does "feel" mean?   To touch.
   b. What does "field" mean?   Open land.

4. a. How do you spell "while"?   W - H - I - L - E.
   b. How do you spell "wild"?   W - I - L - D.

5. a. What does "sold" mean?   The past of "sell."
   b. What does "sole" mean?   The bottom of a shoe.

6. a. What does "goal" mean?   Winning a point in soccer.
   b. What does "gold" mean?   A yellow metal.

7. a. What does "coal" mean?   A black rock that burns.
   b. What does "cold" mean?   The opposite of "hot."

8. a. What does "mild" mean?   Not strong.
   b. What does "mile" mean?   Five thousand two hundred and eighty feet.

9. a. How do you spell "smile"?   S - M - I - L - E.
   b. How do you spell "smiled"?   S - M - I - L - E - D.

10. a. What does "smiled" mean?   The past of "smile."
    b. What does "smile" mean?   To turn up the sides of your lips.

⌒D Pair work: Present and past

1 Listen. Then say these words until you can say them easily.

Present	Past
every day	yesterday
every week	last week
usually	last year
often	two days ago
always	last night

2 Student A: Say sentence **a** or sentence **b**.

Student B: Say words from the box above to complete the sentence.

Take turns saying sentences.

Examples

Student A: I call home.

Student B: Every day.

Student B: We filled the gas tank.

Student A: Yesterday.

1. a. I called home.

b. I call home.

2. a. We filled the gas tank.

b. We fill the gas tank.

3. a. We sail on the lake.

b. We sailed on the lake.

4. a. Babies spill milk.

b. Babies spilled milk.

5. a. The boys fail every test.

b. The boys failed every test.

6. a. They smile a lot.

b. They smiled a lot.

7. a. I mailed a letter.

b. I mail a letter.

8. a. They spelled all the words.

b. They spell all the words.

Music of English

Listen. Then repeat each sentence until you can say it easily.

F Pair work: Did you say "made"?

Student A: Say a word from the list of words below.

Student B: Pretend you heard a different word and ask, "Did you say '. . .'?"

Student A: Correct Student B and answer, "No, I said '. . . .'"

Take turns saying the words.

Examples

Student A: Mail.

Student B: Did you say "made"?

Student A: No, I said "mail."

Student B: Field.

Student A: Did you say "feel"?

Student B: No, I said "field."

Words

mail	made	feel	field
spell	spelled	bowl	bold
pull	pulled	while	wild
sail	sailed	goal	gold

⌒G Linking stop sounds to vowels ᏻᏻᏻ

In English, the stop sounds are **/p/**, **/b/**, **/t/**, **/d/**, **/k/**, and **/g/**.
A stop sound links to a vowel at the beginning of the next word.

1 Listen to the final sounds in words that end in the stop sounds **/t/** and **/d/**.
Then say each sentence until you can say it easily.

1. We paid it.   We paidit .

2. Sit on it.   Siton it.

3. Hold it.   Holdit .

4. Find it.   Findit .

5. Is it cold or hot?   Is it coldor hot?

6. We had a lot of money.   We hada   lotof money.

2 Listen to the final sounds **/b/**, **/p/**, **/k/**, and **/g/**. Then say each sentence until
you can say it easily.

1. The cab is coming.   The cabis coming.

2. I want a tub of butter.   I want a tubof butter.

3. Ask everybody.   Askeverybody .

4. Cook all the food.   Cookall the food.

5. Thank you.   Thankyou .

6. Link all vowels.   Linkall vowels.

7. Help us.   Helpus .

8. A cup of coffee, please.   A cupof coffee, please.

9. Stop it.   Stopit .

10. Tap each syllable.   Tapeach syllable.

11. We keep all mail.   We keepall mail.

12. This is a bag of oranges.   This is a bagof oranges.

What is it?
Where is it?

A Final sounds /t/, /d/, and /r/

1 Look at these pictures.

Stop sounds /t/ and /d/	**Continuing sound /r/**

Looking to the front

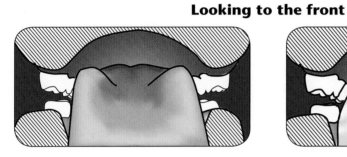

Looking down

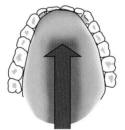
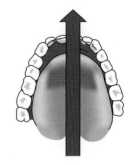

Looking from the side

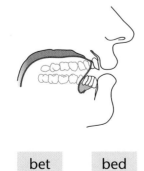

bet	bed		bearrr

2 Listen for the final sounds. Do not say the words.

	STOP	→
1.	bad	bar
	bad	barrr
2.	fat	far
	fat	farrr
3.	feed	fear
	feed	fearrr
4.	fade	fair
	fade	fairrr
5.	card	car
	card	carrr
6.	art	are
	art	arrre
7.	what	where
	what	wherrre

🎧 B Which word do you hear?

1 Listen. Circle the word you hear.

	STOP	→	
1.	(bed)	bear	(bed)
2.	art	are	
3.	card	car	
4.	shared	share	
5.	fired	fire	
6.	what	where	
7.	hired	hire	
8.	feared	fear	
9.	poured	pour	
10.	feet	fear	

2 Listen again.

C Which word is different?

1 Listen to three words. One word is different. Mark it.

	X	Y	Z	
1.	....	....	......✔........	(bed, bed, bear)
2.	....	....	....	
3.	....	....	....	
4.	....	....	....	
5.	....	....	....	
6.	....	....	....	
7.	....	....	....	
8.	....	....	....	

2 Listen again.

D Saying final sounds /t/, /d/, and /r/

Listen. Then say each word until you can say it easily.

STOP	➡
1. fat	far
2. cat	car
3. tide	tire
4. fade	fair
5. paid	pair
6. what	where
7. card	car
8. art	are
9. feared	fear
10. cared	care

E Pair work: Present and past

Present	Past
every day	yesterday
every week	last week
usually	last year
often	two days ago
always	last night

Student A: Say sentence **a** or sentence **b**.

Student B: Say words from the box above to complete the sentences.

Take turns saying the sentences.

Examples

Student A: They shared everything.
Student B: Yesterday.

Student B: I care about my work.
Student A: Always.

1. a. They share everything.
   b. They shared everything.

2. a. I care about my work.
   b. I cared about my work.

3. a. They prepare their lessons.
   b. They prepared their lessons.

4. a. They feared everything.
   b. They fear everything.

5. a. We repaired cars.
   b. We repair cars.

6. a. Snakes scared me.
   b. Snakes scare me.

7. a. I adore her.
   b. I adored her.

F Linking with /r/ 🔗

The sound **/r/** is a continuing sound. It links to a vowel. It also links to another continuing sound at the beginning of the next word.

1 Listen. Then say these words until you can say them easily.

far away	farrʳaway
hear me	hearrʳme
Peter knows	Peterrʳknows

2 Listen. Then say each sentence until you can say it easily.

1. He is far away. He is farrʳaway .
2. Where is it?   Whererʳis it?
3. What are all those things? What arerʳall those things?
4. Peter knows the answer.   Peterrʳknows the answer.
5. Did you hear me? Did you hearrʳme ?
6. Are many people going?   Arerʳmany people going?
7. Her voice is beautiful.   Herrʳvoice is beautiful.
8. You're an hour late.   Yourerʳan   hourrʳlate .

G Linking with /r/, /t/, /d/, and /l/ 🔗

Listen. Then say each sentence until you can say it easily.

1. I had a sandwich. I hada sandwich.
2. Will everybody come?   Willlleverybody come?
3. Where are you?   Whererʳarerʳyou ?
4. What is it?   Whatis it?
5. I heard everything. I heardeverything .
6. Is it hard or soft? Is it hardor soft?
7. The letter never arrived. The letterrʳneverrʳarrived .
8. Jill is reading.   Jillllis reading.
9. We care about our work. We carerʳaboutourrʳwork .
10. Put your hat on. Put your haton .

H Pair work: What does "roar" mean?

Student A: Ask question **a** or question **b**.

Student B: Answer.

Student A: If the answer is correct, say "Right." If it is wrong, ask again.

Take turns asking the questions.

Examples

Student A: What does "roared" mean?

Student B: The past of "roar."

Student A: Right.

Student B: What does "adore" mean?

Student A: The past of "love."

Student B: No. What does "adore" mean?

Student A: To love.

1. a. What does "roar" mean?   The noise of a lion.
    b. What does "roared" mean?   The past of "roar."

2. a. What does "adore" mean?   To love.
    b. What does "adored" mean?   The past of "love."

3. a. What does "repair" mean?   To fix.
    b. What does "repaired" mean?   The past of "repair."

4. a. How do you spell "feared"?   F - E - A - R - E - D.
    b. How do you spell "fear"?   F - E - A - R.

5. a. How do you spell "art"?   A - R - T.
    b. How do you spell "are"?   A - R - E.

6. a. What does "pair" mean?   Two.
    b. What does "paid" mean?   The past of "pay."

7. a. How do you spell "her"?   H - E - R.
    b. How do you spell "hurt"?   H - U - R - T.

8. a. How do you spell "fire"?   F - I - R - E.
   b. How do you spell "fight"?   F - I - G - H - T.

9. a. What does "near" mean?   Not far.
   b. What does "neat" mean?   Not messy.

10. a. How do you spell "tire"?   T - I - R - E.
    b. How do you spell "tight"?   T - I - G - H - T.

I Music of English

Listen. Then repeat each sentence until you can say it easily.

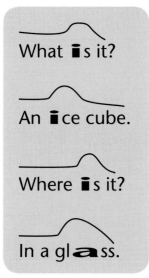

What **i**s it?

An **i**ce cube.

Where **i**s it?

In a gl**a**ss.

J Pair work: What is it? Where is it?

Student A: Point to a picture on the next page and ask, "What is it?"
            or "Where is it?"

Student B: Say an answer from the list on the next page.

Take turns asking the questions.

Examples

Student A: (Point to the elephant.) What is it?
Student B: An elephant.

Student B: Where is it?
Student A: In a zoo.

What?	**Where?**
A cat.	On a chair.
An elephant.	Under a sofa.
An ice cube.	On a desk.
A flag.	On a flagpole.
A jacket.	In a zoo.
A pot.	In a glass.
A computer.	On a stove.

K Music of English

Listen. Then repeat each sentence until you can say it easily.

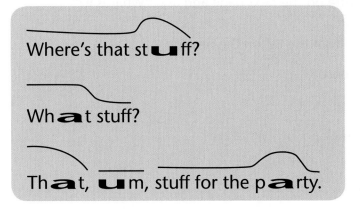

Where's that st **u** ff?

Wh **a** t stuff?

Th **a** t, **u** m, stuff for the p **a** rty.

L Pair work: Asking for more information

1 Listen.

2 Say the conversation with a partner. Take turns as Sue and Joe.
The most important words are in bold.

Joe: Where's the **meat**?

Sue: **What** meat?

Joe: The **chicken**.

Sue: **What** chicken?

Joe: The chicken I put in the **fridge**.

Sue: **When**?

Joe: Last **week**.

Sue: Oh, was that **chicken**? I threw it **away**!

M Review: Most important words and strong syllables

Complete the pyramid on the right with your partner.

1. Find the most important word in the word group at the bottom of the pyramid.
Write that word in the orange level.

2. Find the strong syllable in that word, and write it in the green level.

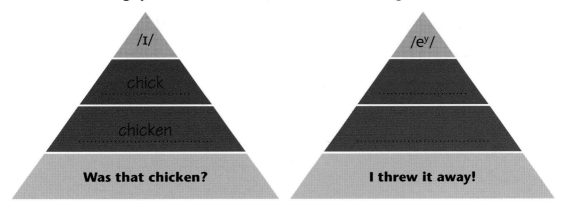

/ɪ/

chick

chicken

Was that chicken?

/eʸ/

I threw it away!

What's a bank for?
Where's the library? It's on Main Street.

A Review: Final sounds /t/, /d/, /s/, and /z/

Listen. Then say these words until you can say them easily.

STOP   **→**

1. but   bus
   but   busss

2. it   is
   it   izzz

3. had   has
   had   hazzz

B Do you hear a final /s/ or /z/ sound?

1 Listen. Mark Yes or No.

	Yes	No	
1.	✔	....	(bus)
2.	....	....	
3.	....	....	
4.	....	....	
5.	....	....	
6.	....	....	
7.	....	....	
8.	....	....	
9.	....	....	
10.	....	....	

2 Listen again.

∩ C Stop sounds + /s/ or /z/

1 Listen. Circle the word you hear.

STOP	**STOP** + /s/ or /z/
1. cab	(cabs)
cab	cabzzz
2. bank	banks
bank	banksss
3. bag	bags
bag	bagzzz
4. stop	stops
stop	stopsss
5. supermarket	supermarkets
supermarket	supermarketsss
6. laundromat	laundromats
laundromat	laundromatsss
7. road	roads
road	roadzzz
8. street	streets
street	streetsss
9. shop	shops
shop	shopsss
10. parking lot	parking lots
parking lot	parking lotsss

2 Listen again.

🎧 D Continuing sounds + /s/ or /z/

1 Listen. Circle the word you hear.

→	→ + /s/ or /z/
1. (plan)	plans
plannn	planzzz
2. school	schools
schoolll	schoolzzz
3. hospital	hospitals
hospitalll	hospitalzzz
4. store	stores
storrr	storezzz
5. theater	theaters
theaterrr	theaterzzz
6. toy	toys
toyyy	toyzzz
7. city	cities
cityyy	citiezzz
8. avenue	avenues
avenuuu	avenuezzz
9. drive	drives
drivvv	drivezzz
10. alley	alleys
alleyyy	alleyzzz

2 Listen again.

E Pair work: Is it one or more than one?

Student A: Say a word from the list of places below.

Student B: If you hear a word meaning one place, hold up one finger. If you hear a word meaning more than one place, hold up all five fingers.

Student A: If the answer is correct, say, "Right." If it is wrong, say the word again.

Take turns saying the words.

Examples

Student A: Banks.

Student B: (Hold up all five fingers.)

Student A: Right.

Student B: Hospitals.

Student A: (Hold up one finger.)

Student B: No, hospitals.

Places

park	parking lot	theaters	parking lots
laundromat	hospitals	school	bookstores
apartments	schools	bank	parks
toy store	drugstore	hospital	bookstore
shopping mall	banks	hotels	office buildings

F Review: Linking with /s/ or /z/ 🔗

Remember that continuing sounds link to vowels and to other continuing sounds.

Listen. Then say each sentence until you can say it easily.

1. The shops are downtown.   The shopsₛₛare downtown.

2. The roads are full of traffic.   The roadzₐₐare full of traffic.

3. The banks are closed today.   The banksₛₛare closed today.

4. Are the shops open?   Are the shopsₛₛopen ?

5. The schools may be open.   The schoolzₐₐmay be open.

6. Cabs never wait here.   Cabzₐₐnever wait here.

7. Two of the shops sell toys.   Two of the shopsₛₛsell toys.

8. All the restaurants serve fast food.   All the restaurantsₛₛserve fast food.

G Music of English 🎵

Listen. Then repeat each sentence until you can say it easily.

What's a b**a**nk for?

It's for saving m**o**ney.

What's a h**o**spital for?

It's for helping s**i**ck people.

H Pair work: What's a bank for?

Student A: Look at the list of places below. Ask what one of the places is for.

Student B: Say an answer from the list of answers below.

Take turns asking the questions.

Example

Student A: What's a library for?

Student B: It's for borrowing books.

Places

park	supermarket	hospital
bank	toy store	high school
drugstore	bakery	preschool
laundromat	library	post office
bookstore	electronics store	parking lot
restaurant	hardware store	office supply store

Answers

It's for eating.	It's for mail.
It's for washing clothes.	It's for saving money.
It's for buying books.	It's for buying office supplies.
It's for buying toys.	It's for borrowing books.
It's for buying stuff like tools.	It's for helping sick people.
It's for buying food.	It's for teaching teenagers.
It's for buying stuff like medicine.	It's for teaching small children.
It's for having picnics.	It's for leaving your car.
It's for buying stuff like computers.	It's for buying baked goods.

🎧 I Music of English 🎵

Listen. Then repeat each sentence until you can say it easily.

Excuse me, where's the library?

It's on Main Street.

Thank you.

No problem.

🎧 J Pair work: Giving locations

1 Listen. Find the places on the map below.

Visitor:	Excuse me, where's the bookstore?
Resident:	It's on the corner of Main and Jen.
Visitor:	Is it near the library?
Resident:	Yes, it's just across the street.
Visitor:	And where is Jen Street?
Resident:	It's one block south of Jean Street.
Visitor:	Thanks a lot for your help.
Resident:	No problem.

2 Say the conversation with a partner. Take turns as the visitor and the resident.

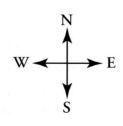

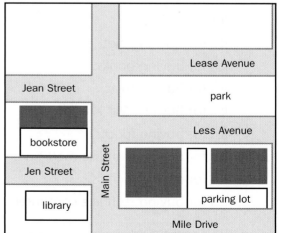

3 Listen. Then take turns saying each of these sample locations to your partner.

1. It's two blocks south of Lease.
2. It's one block west of Mace Avenue.
3. It's across the street from the bookstore.
4. It's on the corner of Jean and Main.
5. It's next to the parking lot.
6. It's between Mile Drive and Mann Street.

K Game: Map challenge EXTRA

1 Student A: Cover Map B on page 93 with a piece of paper, and look at Map A on page 92.

Student B: Cover Map A on page 92 with a piece of paper, and look at Map B on page 93.

2 Student A: Ask the location of a place listed in the box below Map A.

3 Student B: Look at Map B. Answer the question. Use sentences like the ones you just practiced saying in Task J.

4 Student A: Write the place on Map A.

5 Take turns asking the questions. When your maps are complete, check your answers.

Example

Student A: (Look at Map A.) Where's the toy store?
Student B: (Look at Map B.) It's on the corner of Main Street and Jean Street.
Student A: (Write "toy store" on your map.)

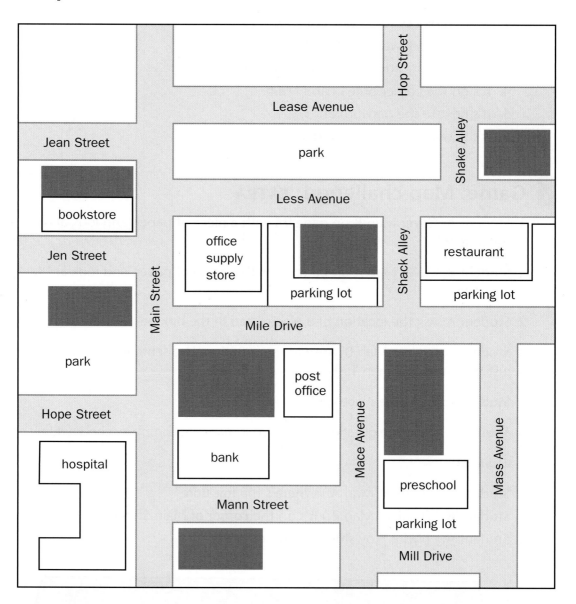

Student A: Ask the location of the places in the box.

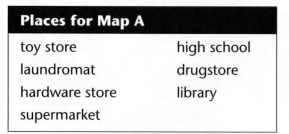

Places for Map A

toy store	high school
laundromat	drugstore
hardware store	library
supermarket	

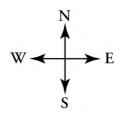

Map B

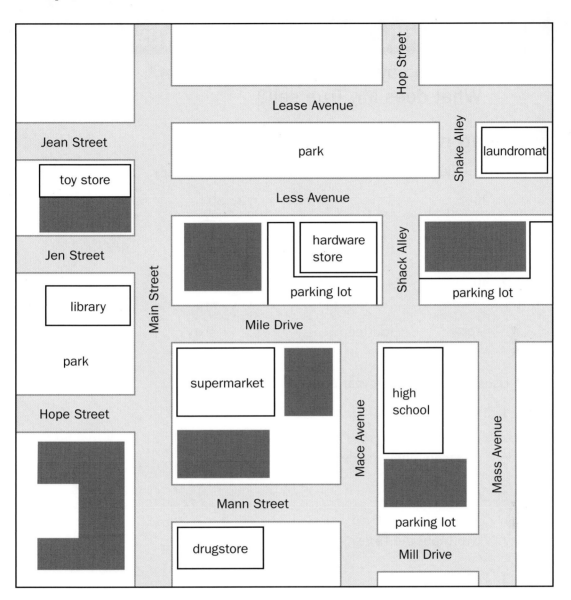

Student B: Ask the location of the places in the box.

Places for Map B	
bookstore	office supply store
hospital	preschool
restaurant	bank
post office	

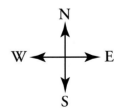

13 Numbers
Checking and Correcting Mistakes

Did you say "ninety"? No, "nineteen."
What does Mr. True sell?

🎧 A Saying numbers and years

1 Listen. Then say each number until you can say it easily.

1. 30   13   **3.** 50   15

thirty   thirteen   fifty   fifteen

2. 40   14   **4.** 60   16

forty   fourteen   sixty   sixteen

2 Listen. Then say each year until you can say it easily.

1. 1999

nineteen ninety-nine

2. 2005

two thousand five

3. 2012

two thousand twelve   *or*   twenty twelve

4. 2029

two thousand twenty-nine   *or*   twenty twenty-nine

B Music of English

Listen. Then repeat each sentence until you can say it easily.

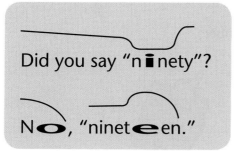

Did you say "n**i**nety"?

N**o**, "ninet**ee**n."

C Pair work: Correcting a mistake about a number

Student A: Say a number from the list of numbers below.

Student B: Check to be sure, but say the wrong number.

Student A: Correct the mistake.

Take turns saying the numbers.

Examples

Student A: Fifty.
Student B: Did you say "fif**teen**"?
Student A: No, "**fif**ty."

Student B: Twenty-nine.
Student A: Did you say "twenty-**five**"?
Student B: No, "twenty-**nine**."

Numbers

13	30	18	80
14	40	19	90
15	50	25	29
16	60	66	67
17	70	98	99

 D Listening for pauses in telephone numbers

Telephone numbers are said with a pause (silence) after each group of numbers. In different countries, these groups are different.

Listen for the pauses in these telephone numbers.

Australia	03-8671-1400
Canada	604-555-5808
Mexico	55-53-36-46-56
New Zealand	64-9-321-5647
United Kingdom	020-7946-0138
United States	212-555-3900

E Saying telephone numbers

1 Listen. Then say these telephone numbers until you can say them easily. The first two phone numbers have area codes.

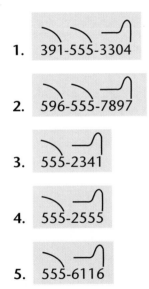

1. 391-555-3304

2. 596-555-7897

3. 555-2341

4. 555-2555

5. 555-6116

2 Now dictate your own telephone number, or one that you choose, to a partner. Check what your partner wrote.

F Stores at the Seaside Mall

1 Read the Seaside Mall directory below. There are three levels, A, B, and C.

2 Listen. Then say the name of each store until you can say it easily.

★ ★ ★
Seaside Mall
DIRECTORY

Men	Location	Phone
Mr. True	1A	555-1698
Big Guy	25B	555-1697

Women		
Allen's Department Store	14C	555-2134
Smart Woman	20A	555-1597

Boys		
Red Dog	16A	555-1718

Girls		
Little Princess	17A	555-1719
California Girl	15A	555-9070

Food		
FastBurger	5B	555-1232
Sunshine Café	6C	555-1658
The Elephant Eatery	7B	555-2194

Other Stores		
Small World	15B	555-3200
Gemstones	13B	555-3214
The Old Oak	21C	555-5599
Speed Electronics	31C	555-8790

G Music of English 🎵

Listen. Then repeat each sentence until you can say it easily.

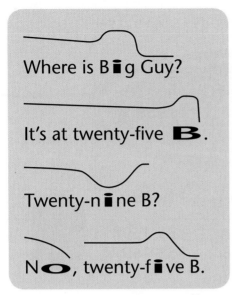

Where is B**i**g Guy?

It's at twenty-five **B**.

Twenty-n**i**ne B?

N**o**, twenty-f**i**ve B.

H Pair work: Calling for information

1 Listen to this phone conversation. A customer is calling for information.

2 Say the conversation with a partner. Take turns as the information clerk and the customer.

Information Clerk:	Seaside Mall. May I help you?
Customer:	Yes, please. What's the telephone number for the Sunshine Café?
Information Clerk:	555-1658.
Customer:	555-1698?
Information Clerk:	No, 555-1658.
Customer:	OK. Where is it?
Information Clerk:	It's at 6C.
Customer:	Thanks.
Information Clerk:	You're welcome. Have a nice day!

I Pair work: Where is it? What's the telephone number?

Customer: Look at the list of places below. (Don't look at the Seaside Mall directory on page 97.) Ask for the location and telephone number of a store.

Information Clerk: Look at the directory on page 97. Answer.

Customer: Check the answer with your partner. Then write the location and telephone number in the box.

Take turns as the customer and the information clerk.

Example

Customer: Excuse me, where is Mr. True?

Information Clerk: It's at 1A.

Customer: Thanks. What's the phone number?

Information Clerk: It's 555-1698.

Customer: 555-1698?

Information Clerk: That's right.

Places

	Location	Phone
Mr. True	1A	555-1698
Big Guy		
Allen's Department Store		
Smart Woman		
Red Dog		
Little Princess		
California Girl		
FastBurger		
Sunshine Café		
The Elephant Eatery		
Small World		
Gemstones		
The Old Oak		
Speed Electronics		

∩ J About the stores at the Seaside Mall

Listen to information about the stores at the Seaside Mall.

SEASIDE MALL

$$$ Expensive		$$ Moderate	$ Inexpensive
$$	Allen's Department Store	clothes, shoes, and cosmetics for women	
$	Big Guy	clothes for men	
$	California Girl	clothes for teenage girls	
$	FastBurger	burgers and ice cream	
$$$	Gemstones	jewelry	
$$	Little Princess	clothes for girls	
$$$	Mr. True	clothes for men	
$$$	Red Dog	clothes for boys	
$$	Small World	toys	
$	Smart Woman	clothes for women	
$$$	Speed Electronics	computers and electronic gadgets	
$$$	Sunshine Café	big sandwiches	
$$	The Elephant Eatery	soups, salads, and pizza	
$$	The Old Oak	books	

∩ K Music of English

Listen. Then repeat each sentence until you can say it easily.

What does Mr. True sell?

Clothes for men.

Did you say clothes for teens?

No, for men.

L Pair work: Checking information

1 Listen to the conversation.

2 Say the conversation two times with a partner.

Customer:	What does California Girl sell?
Information Clerk:	Clothes for teenage girls.
Customer:	Not for **women**?
Information Clerk:	No, for **girls**.
Customer:	Is it expensive?
Information Clerk:	No. It's rather **in**expensive.
Customer:	Thanks.
Information Clerk:	You're very welcome. Have a nice day!

3 Take turns as the customer and the clerk. Ask what a store sells and if it is expensive. Find the answers in Task J on page 100.

M More linking

Listen. Then say each sentence until you can say it easily.

1. Continuing sound + vowel sound

Smart Woman is inexpensive.	Smart Womannnizzzinexpensive .
FastBurger opens at ten.	FastBurgerrropenzzzat ten.

2. Stop sound + vowel sound

The Old Oak is closed on Sundays.	The OldOakis closedon Sundays.
Small World is fun.	Small Worldis fun.

3. Continuing sound + continuing sound

FastBurger never costs much.	FastBurgerrrnever costs much.
Teens like shopping.	Teenzzzlike shopping.
Speed Electronics sells computers.	Speed Electronicssssells computers.

4. Vowel sound + vowel sound

Sunshine Café is expensive.	Sunshine Caféizzz expensive.
Big Guy is always busy.	Big Guyizzz always busy.

5. Same sound to same sound

Gemstones sells jewelry.	Gemstonessssells jewelry.
Mr. Allen never eats lunch.	Mr. Allennnever eats lunch.

N Review: Correcting mistakes

Look at the sentences under each pyramid.

1. Find the most important word and write it in the orange level.

2. Find the strong syllable of that word and write it in the green level.

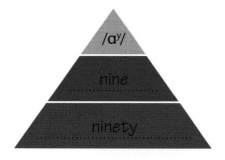

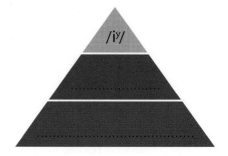

1. Did you say "ninety"?

2. No, "nineteen."

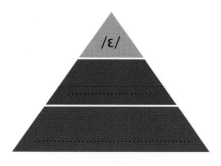

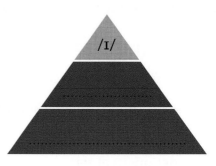

3. Is it expensive?

4. No, inexpensive.

14

Final Sounds /n/, /l/, /nd/, and /ld/
Linking with /n/, /l/, /nd/, and /ld/

What's a trail?
It's a path.

A Final sounds /n/, /l/, and /d/

Look at these pictures.

/l/	/n/	/d/

Looking from the side

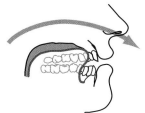

Air continues out of the mouth

Air continues out of the nose only

Air stops

Looking to the front

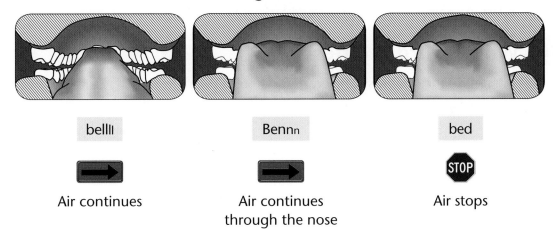

bell**ll**

Ben**nn**

bed

Air continues

Air continues through the nose

Air stops

B Listening for final sounds /n/ and /l/

Listen to the final sound of each word. Do not say the words.

1. mine   mile
2. nine   Nile
3. can   call
4. ten   tell
5. man   mall
6. win   will
7. pin   pill
8. when   well

C Which word do you hear?

1 Listen. Circle the word you hear.

1. (bone)   bowl   (bone)
2. rain   rail
3. main   mail
4. when   well
5. fine   file
6. pain   pail
7. train   trail
8. ten   tell

2 Listen again.

D Which word is different?

1 Listen to three words. One word is different. Mark it.

	X	Y	Z	
1.	....	✔	....	(ten, tell, ten)
2.	....	....	....	
3.	....	....	....	
4.	....	....	....	
5.	....	....	....	
6.	....	....	....	
7.	....	....	....	
8.	....	....	....	

2 Listen again.

E Saying final sounds /n/ and /l/

Listen. Then say each word until you can say it easily.

1.	pin	pill	**6.**	main	mail
2.	win	will	**7.**	cone	coal
3.	bone	bowl	**8.**	when	well
4.	rain	rail	**9.**	then	they'll
5.	can	call	**10.**	train	trail

F Saying final sounds /nd/ and /ld/

Listen. Then say each word until you can say it easily.

1. find   filed
2. phoned   fold
3. trained   trailed
4. mind   mild
5. spend   spelled
6. owned   old

G Music of English

Listen. Then repeat each sentence until you can say it easily. Be careful with the final sounds in the most important words.

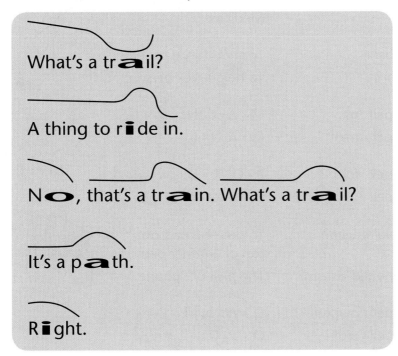

H Pair work: What's a train for?

Student A: Ask question **a** or question **b**.
Student B: Answer.
Student A: If the answer is correct, say "Right." If it is wrong, ask again.

Take turns asking the questions.

Example

Student A: What's a trail?
Student B: A thing to ride in.
Student A: No, what's a **trail**?
Student B: It's a path.
Student A: Right.

1. a. What's a trail?   A path.
    b. What's a train?   A thing to ride in.

2. a. What's a trail for?   To walk on.
    b. What's a train for?   To ride in.

3. a. How do you spell "trail"?   T - R - A - I - L.
    b. How do you spell "train"?   T - R - A - I - N.

4. a. What's a pin?   A sharp thing.
    b. What's a pill?   Medicine.

5. a. What's a pin for?   To stick things together.
    b. What's a pill for?   To help a sick person.

6. a. How do you spell "main"?   M - A - I - N.
    b. How do you spell "mail"?   M - A - I - L.

7. a. How do you spell "fold"?   F - O - L - D.
    b. How do you spell "phoned"?   P - H - O - N - E - D.

8. a. What does "fold" mean?   To put one part on
                                  top of another part.

    b. What does "phoned" mean? The past of "phone."

9. a. How do you spell "owned"?   O - W - N - E - D.
    b. How do you spell "old"?   O - L - D.

I Linking with /l/, /n/, /ld/, and /nd/ 🔗

1 Listen. Then say these words until you can say them easily.

Call our friends.   Calllour friends.

Hold on.   Holdon .

Spend it.   Spendit .

phone number   phonennnumber

2 Listen. Then say each sentence until you can say it easily.

1. Please call our friends.   Please calllour friends.

2. We called our boss.   We calledour boss.

3. Hold on tight.   Holdon tight.

4. They can always go.   They cannnalways go.

5. When are you coming?   Whennnare you coming?

6. Don't spend all the money.   Don't spendall the money.

7. She spelled every word right.   She spelledevery word right.

8. What's your phone number?   What's your phonennnumber ?

J Pair work: Checking information

1 Listen to the conversations.

2 Say the conversations with a partner.

1. ***The Emergency***
   Aunt: The baby swallowed a pill!
   Mother: A pin! Call the doctor!
   Aunt: Not a **pin**, a **pill**.
   Mother: Pin or pill, we have to call the doctor!

2. ***The Misunderstanding***
   Father: Did you fold them?
   Son: Fold what?
   Father: The shirts I left for you to fold.
   Son: Did you say "**fold** them"? I thought you said "**Phone** Tim."
   Father: Did you phone Tim?
   Son: Yes! I told him you left some shirts. He thought it was strange!

K The mirror test: Final sounds /n/ and /l/ EXTRA

1 Find a small mirror and follow these steps.

1. Hold the mirror close to your face, under your nose.
2. Say the sound **/n/** strongly.
3. Quickly look at the mirror. You should see a cloud.

nnn

4. Say the word "bone." You should see a cloud again.
5. Say the sound **/l/** strongly. You should not see a cloud.

lll

6. Say the word "bowl." You should not see a cloud.

2 Try the mirror test with the words below. Check your mirror after each word.

cone	coal
seen	seal
ten	tell
can	call
pin	pill

15

Final Sounds /s/, /θ/, and /t/
Linking with /θ/

What's a bath for?
To get clean.

A Final sounds /s/, /θ/, and /t/

1 Look at these pictures.

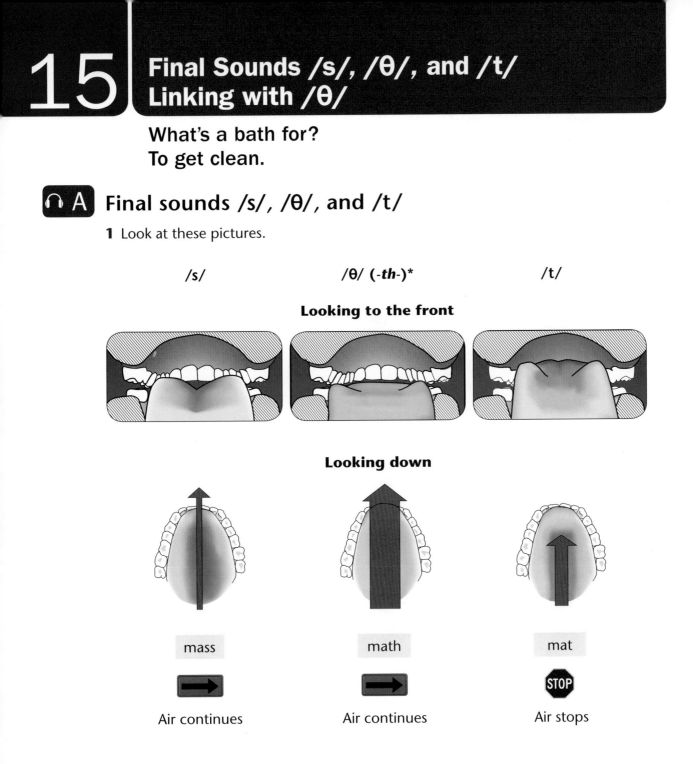

/s/   /θ/ (-*th*-)*   /t/

Looking to the front

Looking down

mass   math   mat

Air continues   Air continues   Air stops

---

* The **/θ/** symbol is one of the International Pronunciation Alphabet (IPA) symbols for the letters
-**th**-. See Key to Sound Symbols on page xvii.

2 Listen for the sound at the end of these words. Do not say the words.

→	→	STOP
mass	math	mat
bass	bath	bat
boss	both	boat

B Which word do you hear?

1 Listen. Circle the word you hear.

→	STOP	
1. (both)	boat	(both)
2. path	pat	
3. mass	mat	
4. Beth	bet	
5. force	fort	
6. nice	night	
7. rice	right	
8. face	fate	
9. with	wit	
10. race	rate	

2 Listen again.

C Which word is different?

1 Listen to three words. One word is different. Mark it.

	X	Y	Z	
1.	....	.......✔........	....	(boat, both, boat)
2.	....	....	....	
3.	....	....	....	
4.	....	....	....	
5.	....	....	....	
6.	....	....	....	
7.	....	....	....	
8.	....	....	....	

2 Listen again.

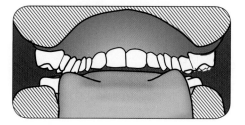 D Saying final /θ/ (-th-)

1 Look again at the picture of how to say /θ/.

2 Listen. Then say each word until you can say it easily.

1. bath
2. both
3. teeth
4. math
5. mouth

E Saying final sounds /θ/, /t/, and /d/ in numbers

Listen. Then say each number until you can say it easily.

1. first	first	
2. second	second	
3. third	third	
4. fourth	fourth_{th th}	
5. fifth	fifth_{th th}	
6. sixth	sixth_{th th}	
7. seventh	seventh_{th th}	
8. eighth	eighth_{th th}	
9. ninth	ninth_{th th}	
10. tenth	tenth_{th th}	

⌢ F Saying final sounds /s/, /z/, /θ/, and /t/

Listen. Then say each word until you can say it easily.

	➡️	➡️	🛑 STOP
	/s/ or /z/	**/θ/**	**/t/**
1.	bass	bath	bat
	bassss	bathth th	bat
2.	mass	math	mat
	massss	maththth	mat
3.	boss	both	boat
	bossss	boththth	boat
4.	fours	fourth	fort
	fourzzz	fourththth	fort

⌢ G Music of English 🎵

Listen. Then repeat each sentence until you can say it easily.

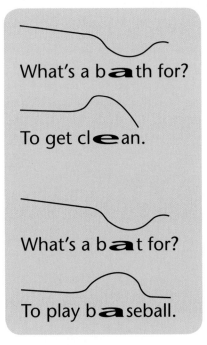

What's a b**a**th for?

To get cl**e**an.

What's a b**a**t for?

To play b**a**seball.

H Pair work: What's a bath for?

Student A: Ask question **a** or question **b**.

Student B: Answer.

Student A: If the answer is correct, say "Right." If it is wrong, ask again.

Take turns asking the questions.

NOTE: The questions continue on the next page.

Examples

Student A: How do you spell "bat"?

Student B: B - A - T - H.

Student A: No. How do you spell "bat"?

Student B: What's a bath for?

Student A: To get clean.

Student B: Right.

1. a. How do you spell "bath"?   B - A - T - H.
   b. How do you spell "bat"?   B - A - T.

2. a. What's a bath for?   To get clean.
   b. What's a bat for?   To play baseball.

3. a. What does "both" mean?   Two things. Not just one of them.
   b. What does "boat" mean?   A small ship.

4. a. What does "bath" mean?   A tub, in the bathroom.
   b. What does "bass" mean?   A kind of fish.

5. a. How do you spell "both"?   B - O - T - H.
   b. How do you spell "boat"?   B - O - A - T.

6. a. What does "math" mean?   Work with numbers.
   b. What does "mat" mean?   A small rug.

7. a. How do you say M - A - T - H? "Math."
   b. How do you say M - A - S - S? "Mass."

8. a. What does "mouse" mean?   A small animal.
   b. What does "mouth" mean?   It's used for eating and speaking.

9. a. What comes after "night"?   Day.
   b. What comes after "ninth"?   Tenth.

10. a. What's a path?   A small trail.
    b. What's a pass?   A free ticket.

I   Pair work: Checking days and dates

Student A: Say a day, month, and date from the list below.

Student B: Check what your partner said.

Student A: If the answer is correct, say "Yes." If it is wrong, give the correct answer.

Take turns saying the days and dates.

Examples

Student A: Tuesday, March first.

Student B: Did you say "Thursday"?

Student A: No, "Tuesday."

Student B: Monday, April fourth.

Student A: Did you say "April fourth"?

Student B: Yes.

Day	Month	Date
Monday	January	first
Tuesday	February	second
Wednesday	March	third
Thursday	April	fourth
Friday	May	fifth
Saturday	June	sixth
Sunday	July	seventh
	August	eighth
	September	ninth
	October	tenth
	November	
	December	

∩ J Linking with /θ/ 🔗

1 Listen to these groups of words.

both of them	boththth of them
Fourth of July	Fourththth of July
math and English	maththth and English
both things	boththth things

2 Listen. Then say each sentence until you can say it easily.

1. I want a bath after dinner. I want a baththth after dinner.

2. It was the Fourth of July. It was the Fourththth of July.

3. Both of them came. Boththth of them came.

4. Sue is studying math and English. Sue is studying maththth and English.

5. Her teeth are very white. Her teethth th are very white.

6. The path over the mountain is hard. The paththth over the mountain is hard.

7. The path through the woods is easy. The paththth through the woods is easy.

8. We both think you should come. We boththth th think you should come.

9. They both thank you. They boththth th thank you.

10. He left both things at home. He left boththth th things at home.

K Review: Linking 🔗

Listen. Then say each sentence until you can say it easily.

1. Continuing sound + vowel sound

When is the store open? | Whenₙis the storeᵣopen ?

Will it open before eight? | Willₗit open beforeᵣeight ?

2. Stop sound + vowel sound

The bank opens at eight. | The bankopens ateight .

I'd like a cup of tea. | I'd likea cupof tea.

3. Continuing sound + continuing sound

She wants fish. | She wantsₛfish .

The store's near Main. | The storezzznearᵣᵣMain .

4. Vowel sound + vowel sound.

Does he ever drink coffee or tea? | Does heₑever drink coffeeₑor tea?

Make the dog go away. | Make the dog gooₒaway .

She adores vanilla ice cream. | Sheₑadorez vanillaₐice cream.

5. Same sound + same sound

Will Lucy arrive soon? | WillₗLucy arrive soon?

Please stop pushing! | PleasezzstoppushinG !

6. Linking a group of words

Go away! Far away! | Gooₒaway ! Farᵣᵣaway !

Come again whenever you want to. | Comemₘagain wheneverᵣᵣyou wantto .

Will it open at ten? | Willₗitopennₙatten ?

Will it open before nine? | Willₗitopen beforeᵣᵣnine ?

Bob ate all of the fish soup. | Bobatealllₗof the fishshₛₕsoup .

16 | Review

🎧 A Counting syllables: The Sunshine Café ☐ ☐ ☐

1 Listen to the menu for the Sunshine Café.

Sunshine Café
THESE SANDWICHES ARE AN ADVENTURE

The San Francisco
Fish, avocado, lettuce, tomatoes, and artichoke

The Dallas
Barbecued beef, hot peppers, and onions

The Honolulu
Roasted chicken, pineapple, red onions, and mayonnaise

The New York
Corned beef, pickles, tomatoes, and mustard

The Toronto
Smoked chicken, roasted bell peppers, and cream cheese

The L.A.
Cheese, sun-dried tomatoes, cucumbers, and butter

Plain Sandwiches
Peanut butter and jelly
Tuna salad
Egg salad
Choice of freshly baked bread
white, whole wheat, rye, French roll

Beverages
Coffee, tea, iced tea, milk, lemonade, juice, sparkling water

2 Fill in the blank lines below.

1. Write the name of one of the sandwiches. ....

2. How many syllables are in the name of this sandwich? ....

3. How many syllables are in the first food in the sandwich? ....

4. Which beverage has the most syllables? ....

5. How many syllables does it have? ....

3 Check your answers with a partner.

B Sounds and syllables chart

Write one word from the menu in each box in the chart. Some words belong in more than one box, so you can use the same word in two places.

	One syllable	Two syllables	Three syllables
Two Vowel Rule Underline the alphabet vowel.	b_a_ked	r_o_asted	artich_o_ke
One Vowel Rule Underline the relative vowel.	f_i_sh	p_e_ppers	l_e_monade
Strong syllables Underline the strong syllable.	<u>white</u>	<u>pep</u>pers	<u>sand</u>wiches
Final stop sounds Underline the final stop sound.	ho_t_	mustar_d_	articho_k_e
Final continuing sounds Underline the final continuing sound.	be_ll_	chicke_n_	mayonnai_s_e

Listen. Then say the conversation until you can say it easily.

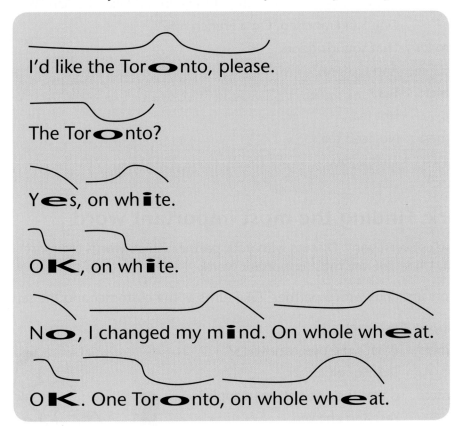

I'd like the Tor⬤nto, please.

The Tor⬤nto?

Y⬤s, on wh▮te.

O◤K, on wh▮te.

N⬤, I changed my m▮nd. On whole wh⬤at.

O◤K. One Tor⬤nto, on whole wh⬤at.

🎧 D **Pair work: The most important word**

1 Listen to these conversations. Underline the most important word in each word group.

2 Say the conversations with a partner. Take turns as the customer and the server.

NOTE: the second conversation is on the next page.

1. Customer: I'd like the Toronto, please.
   Server: The Toronto?
   Customer: Yes, on whole wheat.
   Server: OK. One Toronto, on whole wheat. Coming right up!

2. Customer: I'd like the Honolulu, please.

   Server: OK, one Honolulu. What kind of bread?

   Customer: Whole wheat. No, I changed my mind. I'd like the San Francisco.

   Server: One San Francisco. On a French roll?

   Customer: That sounds good.

   Server: And to drink?

   Customer: Tea.

   Server: Hot tea?

   Customer: No, iced tea.

   Server: Thank you.

E Pair work: Finding the most important word

1 Read these conversations. Discuss with your partner which words are most important. Underline the most important words.

2 Say the conversations with a partner. Take turns as the customer and the server.

1. *The Happy Customer*

Customer: What's the best sandwich?

Server: The Honolulu.

Customer: Is that the one with pineapple?

Server: Yes. And chicken.

Customer: Smoked chicken?

Server: No, roasted chicken.

Customer: That sounds fine!

2. *A Problem with Lunch*

Customer: I'd like the San Francisco, please.

Server: No fish today.

Customer: Well, then I'd like the Toronto.

Server: No chicken today.

Customer: Do you have anything?

Server: Cheese. But the cheese is bad.

Customer: Then just bring me coffee.

F Music of English

Listen. Then say the conversation until you can say it easily.

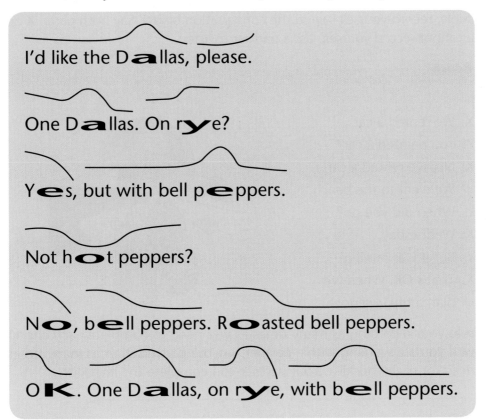

I'd like the D**a**llas, please.

One D**a**llas. On r**y**e?

Y**e**s, but with bell p**e**ppers.

Not h**o**t peppers?

N**o**, b**e**ll peppers. R**o**asted bell peppers.

O**K**. One D**a**llas, on r**y**e, with b**e**ll peppers.

G Working with the pyramid

Complete the two pyramids.

1. Find the most important word of each word group and write it in the orange level.
2. Then find the strong syllable of that word, and write it in the green level.

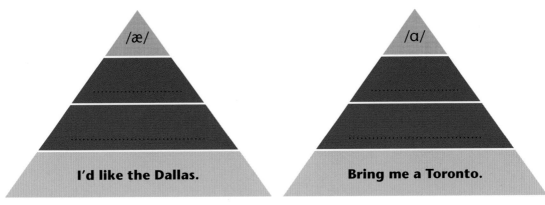

/æ/

I'd like the Dallas.

/ɑ/

Bring me a Toronto.

H Check yourself: Syllables, linking, and most important words

1 If possible, record yourself saying the conversation below. Say both parts, **X** and **Y**. If you cannot record yourself, ask a partner to listen.

The Beach

Line

1 X: We rented a car.

2 Y: You painted a car?

3 X: No, we rented a car.

4   We went to the beach.

5 Y: When did you go?

6 X: Wednesday.

7 Y: But it was raining!

8 X: That's OK. When we

9   plan a trip, we go!

2 Listen to your recording as many times as you need to complete each checklist below. If you are working with a partner, say the conversation as many times as you need for each checklist. Your partner can complete the checklists.

Checklist 1: Syllables ☐ ☐ ☐

Did you get the right number of syllables in these words?

Line		Yes	No	Syllables
1	rented	....	....	(2)
2	painted	....	....	(2)
6	Wednesday	....	....	(2)
7	raining	....	....	(2)
9	plan	....	....	(1)

Checklist 2: Linking

Did you link these words?

Line	Yes	No	
1 rented a	....	....	renteda
2 painted a	....	....	painteda
4 went to	....	....	wentto
7 was raining	....	....	wazzzraining
8 That's OK	....	....	ThatsssOK
9 plan a	....	....	plannna

Checklist 3: Most important words

Did your voice go up or down on these words?

Line	Yes	No	
1 car	....	....	car
2 painted	....	....	painted
3 rented	....	....	rented
4 beach	....	....	beach
5 go	....	....	go
6 Wednesday	....	....	Wednesday
7 raining	....	....	raining
9 plan	....	....	plan
9 go	....	....	go

3 Record the conversation again. Or say it again for your partner.
Listen for your improvement.

I Check yourself: Final sounds, linking, and most important words

1 Record yourself saying the conversation. Say both parts, **X** and **Y**. If you cannot record yourself, ask a partner to listen.

A Party

Line

1 X: We're having a party tomorrow night.
2 Y: What kind of party?
3 X: A birthday party.
4 Y: Who's it for?
5 X: My sister. She's going to be nineteen.
6 Y: Who's coming?
7 X: A lot of people.

2 Listen to your recording as many times as you need to complete each checklist below. If you are working with a partner, say the conversation as many times as you need for each checklist. Your partner can complete the checklists.

Checklist 1: Final sounds

Did you say the final sounds clearly in these words?

Line	Yes	No	
1 We're	....	....	➡️
2 kind	....	....	🛑
4 Who's	....	....	➡️
5 sister	....	....	➡️
5 nineteen	....	....	➡️
7 lot	....	....	🛑

Checklist 2: Linking 🔗🔗🔗

Did you link these words?

Line		Yes	No	
1	having a party	....	....	havingaₐₐparty
1	tomorrow night	....	....	tomorrowwᵥₙight
2	kind of	....	....	kindof
4	Who's it	....	....	Whozzₑit
5	going to	....	....	goingto
5	be nineteen	....	....	beeₑnineteen
7	a lot	....	....	aaₐlot
7	lot of	....	....	lotof

Checklist 3: Most important words

Did your voice go up or down on these words?

Line		Yes	No	
1	party	....	....	p◀rty
2	kind	....	....	k▮nd
3	birthday	....	....	b▮rthday
4	for	....	....	f●r
5	sister	....	....	s▮ster
5	nineteen	....	....	ninet●en
6	coming	....	....	c●ming
7	lot	....	....	l●t

3 Record the conversation again. Or say it again for your partner.
Listen for your improvement.

J Review: Syllables, linking, and most important words

1 Record yourself saying this conversation the same way you did before, or ask a partner to listen.

A Trip in the U.S.A.

Line

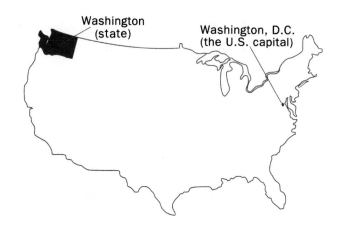

Washington (state)

Washington, D.C. (the U.S. capital)

1 X: I'm planning a trip.

2 Y: A long trip?

3 X: No, just a short one.

4 Y: Where are you going?

5 X: Washington.

6 Y: The capital?

7 X: No, Washington state.

8 Y: That's a long trip!

9 X: Oh, we're flying.

10 So it won't take long.

11 Y: Is this for business?

12 X: No, just for a vacation.

13 Y: Well, have a super trip!

2 Listen to your recording as many times as you need to complete each checklist below. If you are working with a partner, say the conversation as many times as you need for each checklist. Your partner can complete the checklists.

Checklist 1: Syllables ☐ ☐ ☐
Did you get the right number of syllables in these words?

Line		Yes	No	Syllables
1	planning	....	....	(2)
5	Washington	....	....	(3)
6	capital	....	....	(3)
9	flying	....	....	(2)
11	business	....	....	(2)
12	vacation	....	....	(3)
13	super	....	....	(2)

Checklist 2: Linking

Did you link these words?

Line		Yes	No	
3	just a	....	....	justa
4	Where are you	....	....	Whererᴗarerᴗyou
8	That's a	....	....	Thatsssa
12	for a	....	....	forrᴗa
13	have a	....	....	haveᴠᴠa

Checklist 3: Most important word

Did your voice go up or down on these words?

Line		Yes	No	
1	trip	....	....	tr**i**p
2	long	....	....	l**o**ng
3	short	....	....	sh**o**rt
4	going	....	....	g**o**ing
5	Washington	....	....	W**a**shington
6	capital	....	....	c**a**pital
7	state	....	....	st**a**te
8	long	....	....	l**o**ng
9	flying	....	....	fl**y**ing
10	won't	....	....	w**o**n't
11	business	....	....	b**u**siness
12	vacation	....	....	vac**a**tion
13	super	....	....	s**u**per

3 Record the conversation again. Or say it again for your partner. Listen for your improvement.

Appendix A
Parts of the Mouth

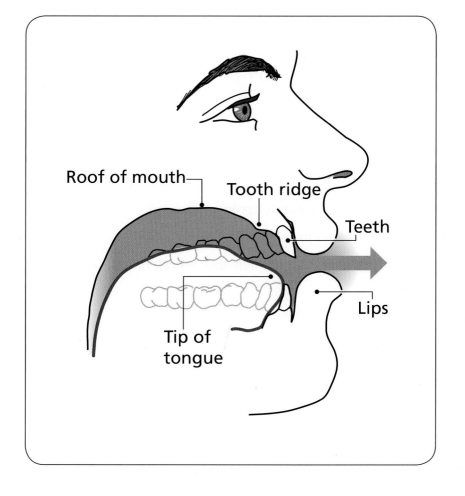

Roof of mouth

Tooth ridge

Teeth

Tip of tongue

Lips

Appendix B
Vowel Rules

A Review of vowel rules

These rules work for many words.

The Two Vowel Rule

When there are two vowel letters in a syllable:

1. The first vowel letter says its alphabet name.

2. The second vowel letter is silent.

This rule is true for many words.

/eʸ/	/iʸ/	/aʸ/	/oʷ/	/uʷ/
cake	tea	ice	cone	cube
remain	repeat	arrive	soapy	excuse

The One Vowel Rule

When there is only one vowel letter in a syllable:

1. The vowel letter says its relative sound.

2. This sound is a relative of the alphabet vowel, but it is not the same sound.

This rule is true for many words.

/æ/	/ɛ/	/ɪ/	/ɑ/	/ʌ/
can	pencil	finger	hot	summer
Mack	Jenny	Kitty	John	Russ

B More words that follow the vowel rules

/eʸ/	/æ/	/iʸ/	/ɛ/	/aʸ/	/ɪ/	/oʷ/	/a/	/uʷ/	/ʌ/
ate	at	read	red	mile	mill	coat	cot	suit	sun
rain	ran	seat	set	file	fill	clothes	cloth	true	run
make	Mac	seal	sell	type	tip	soak	sock	blue	bun
same	Sam	mean	men	time	Tim	note	not	tube	tub
rate	rat	beat	bet	style	still	hope	hop	cue	cup

C The letters -y- and -w- as vowels

1 The letter **-y-** sometimes sounds like /iʸ/.

/iʸ/
- city
- pretty
- silly
- company

- history
- bakery
- electricity
- jewelry

- liberty
- lottery
- comedy

2 The letter **-y-** sometimes sounds like /aʸ/.

/aʸ/
- sky
- why
- try

- fly
- my

- apply
- cry

3 Sometimes the letters **-y-** and **-w-** act like a second vowel when they follow the letter **-a-** or **-o-**. Then the word may follow the Two Vowel Rule.

/eʸ/
- pay
- say
- play
- day

- stay
- tray
- may
- gray

- way
- today
- yesterday

/oʷ/
- show
- slow
- grow
- flow

- below
- throw
- arrow
- low

- snow
- rainbow
- pillow
- know

A The Two Vowel Rule

This rule works for many words, but not all. The chart below shows how often the Two Vowel Rule works in strong syllables. For example, the letters -**ai**- have the /e^y/ sound 95% of the time.

How often does the Two Vowel Rule work?			
Letters	**Sounds**	**Percent of time**[1]	**Examples**
-**ai**- -**a**- + final -**e**- -**ay**-	/e^y/	95% 90% 93%	rain, train, afraid cake, came, ate day, say, play
-**e**- + final -**e**- -**ee**- -**ea**- -**y**-[2]	/i^y/	32% 98% 69% 95%	Pete, these, athlete tree, meet, green tea, please, meat city, funny, lucky
-**i**- + final -**e** -**igh**-[2]	/a^y/	77% 100%	ice, time, fine high, night, light
-**o**- + final -**e** -**oa**- -**ow**-[2]	/o^w/	76% 94% 53%	home, phone, alone coat, soap, coach show, below, follow
-**u**- + final -**e** -**oo**-[2]	/u^w/	94% 88%	cute, blue, flute room, choose, school

[1] Source: *A Survey of English Spelling*, Edward Carney, Routledge, London, 1994. These percentages of times that these spellings produce these vowel sounds are based on analyses of a database of 2.5 million words in British and American dictionaries.

[2] NOTE: -**y**-, -**igh**-, -**ow**-, and -**oo**- do not actually fit the Two Vowel Rule but are included because they are so often pronounced with these vowel sounds.

B The One Vowel Rule

This rule works for many words, but not all. The chart below shows how often the One Vowel Rule works in strong syllables. For example, the letter -a- has the /æ/ sound 91% of the time.

How often does the One Vowel Rule work?			
Letters	**Sounds**	**Percent of time**[1]	**Examples**
-a-	/æ/	91%	has, cat, aspirin, answer
-e-	/ɛ/	82%	bed, message, medicine
-i-	/ɪ/	93%	his, big, simple, children
-o-	/ɑ/	74%	stop, shop, problem
-u-	/ʌ/	66%	up, sun, butter, hundred

---

[1] Source: *A Survey of English Spelling*, Edward Carney, Routledge, London, 1994. These percentages of times that these spellings produce these vowel sounds are based on analyses of a database of 2.5 million words in British and American dictionaries.

Appendix D
Tongue Shapes for
/t/, /d/, /s/, /z/, /θ/, /l/, and /r/

Looking to the front

/t/ and /d/

/s/ and /z/

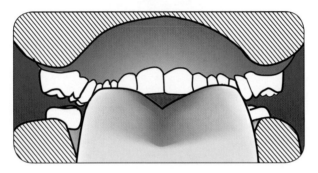

/θ/ (-*th*-)*

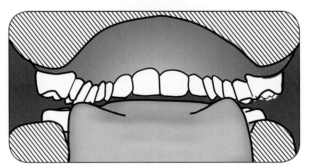

---

* The **/θ/** symbol is one of the International Pronunciation Alphabet (IPA) symbols for the letters -**th**-. See Key to Sound Symbols on page xvii.

/l/

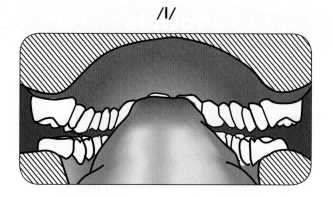

/r/

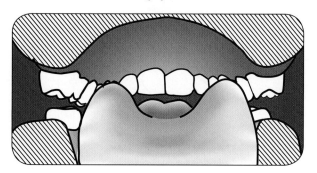

Extra Practice 1
Vowels

🎧 Part 1 The tongue in alphabet vowel sounds

1 Look at these pictures of the tongue pronouncing the alphabet vowel sound for each letter. The solid line in the picture shows where the tongue begins. The dotted line shows how the tongue moves at the end.

2 Listen to the alphabet vowel sounds while you look at each picture.

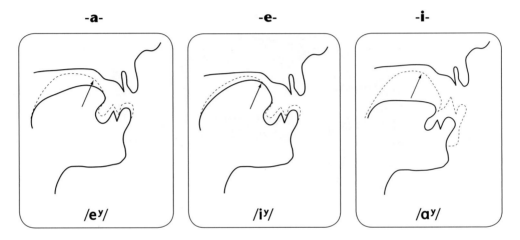

-a- /eʸ/   -e- /iʸ/   -i- /aʸ/

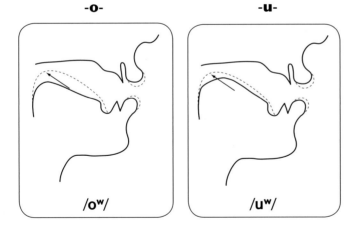

-o- /oʷ/   -u- /uʷ/

🎧 Part 2   The lips in alphabet vowel sounds

The following pictures show how the lips change when the alphabet vowel sounds are being said.

Listen to the alphabet vowel sounds while you look at the pictures.

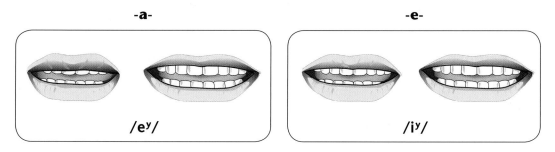

-a- /eʸ/

-e- /iʸ/

-i- /aʸ/

-o- /oʷ/

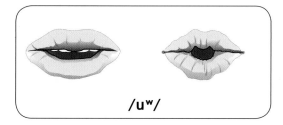

-u- /uʷ/

Part 3   Practicing the vowel rules

 A   The Two Vowel Rule

1 There are two vowel letters in the **first** syllable of the words below. Listen.
Then say each word until you can say it easily.

/eʸ/	/iʸ/	/aʸ/	/oʷ/	/uʷ/
painting	**free**way	**Ice**land	**float**ing	**Tues**day
sailboat	**seat**ed	**pine**apple	**soap**y	**use**ful

NOTE: Some words with the letter **-u-**, like "use," "cube," and "cute," have
a /y/ sound before the /uʷ/ sound. But a simple /uʷ/, in words like "June"
and "rule," is more common.

2 There are two vowel letters in the **last** syllable of the words below. Listen.
Then say each word until you can say it easily.

/eʸ/	/iʸ/	/aʸ/	/oʷ/	/uʷ/
e**rase**	de**lete**	in**side**	a**lone**	intro**duce**
ar**range**	a**sleep**	a**live**	com**pose**	ex**cuse**
ex**plain**	re**peat**	de**fine**	o**ppose**	pro**duce**
de**lay**	su**preme**	re**plied**	a**pproach**	in**clude**

 B   The One Vowel Rule

1 There is one vowel letter in the **first** syllable of the words below. Listen.
Then say each word until you can say it easily.

/æ/	/ɛ/	/ɪ/	/ɑ/	/ʌ/
after	**en**ter	**his**tory	**prob**lem	**ug**ly
master	**yell**ow	**miss**ing	**cop**y	**runn**ing
asking	**tel**evision	**In**ternet	**hot**ter	**Sun**day
Saturday	**rel**ative	**chil**dren	**om**elet	**un**der

2 There is one vowel letter in the **last** syllable of the words below. Listen.
Then say each word until you can say it easily.

/æ/	/ɛ/	/ɪ/	/ɑ/	/ʌ/
a**ttach**	pre**tend**	for**bid**	for**got**	un**plug**
sub**tract**	for**get**	in**sist**	a**dopt**	in**struct**
de**mand**	su**ggest**	be**gin**	a**llot**	be**gun**

Part 1 /v/ and /b/

A Listening to /v/ and /b/

1 Listen to the final sound in each of these words.

   rove   robe   curve   curb

2 Listen to the beginning sound in each of these words.

   vase   base   vote   boat

B Saying /v/ and /b/

The sound **/v/** can continue, but the sound **/b/** is a sound that stops.

1. When saying **/v/**, the upper teeth touch the back of the lower lip. The lips do not touch each other, and this allows air to flow out of the mouth.

2. When saying **/b/**, the lips close, stopping the air inside the mouth.

1 Look at the pictures below to see the differences between **/v/** and **/b/**.

rove /v/   **robe** /b/

Looking from the side

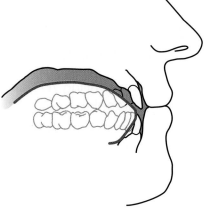

2 Silently try the positions for these two sounds.

NOTE: If you have trouble keeping your lips apart for the /v/ sound, place a pencil or your finger under your upper lip to remind you to keep the lips apart.

3 Practice whispering the words "rove" and "robe." Then practice the words out loud.

⌒C Which word do you hear?

1 Listen. Circle the word you hear.

1. (vase)   base
2. rove   robe
3. van   ban
4. very   berry
5. vote   boat

2 Practice saying the words you circled.

Part 2   /r/ and /l/

⌒A Listening to /r/ and /l/

1 Listen to the final sound in each word.

car   call   tire   tile   fear   feel

2 Listen to the beginning sound in each word.

row   low   rhyme   lime   rain   lane

B Saying /r/ and /l/

The sounds /r/ as in "fear" and /l/ as in "feel" are continuing sounds.

1. When pronouncing /r/, air flows out along the middle of the tongue without stopping.

2. When pronouncing /l/, the tip of the tongue touches the tooth ridge at the front of the mouth, and air flows out each side.

1 Look at the pictures below to see the difference between /r/ and /l/.

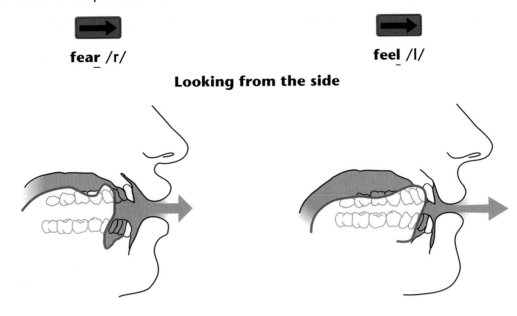

fear /r/   feel /l/

2 Whisper the words "fear" and "feel" several times. Then practice saying them out loud.

🎧 C Which word do you hear?

1 Listen. Circle the word you hear.

Final sound

1. roll   (roar)
2. heal   hear
3. coal   core
4. steel   steer
5. fail   fair

Beginning sound

6. lock   rock
7. low   row
8. late   rate
9. lamb   ram
10. lime   rhyme

2 Practice saying the words you circled.

Part 3 /n/ and /l/

A Listening to /n/ and /l/

1 Listen to the final sound in each word.

    ten   tell   mine   mile   win will

2 Listen to the beginning sound in each word.

    no   low   night light   need lead

B Saying /n/ and /l/

The sounds /n/ and /l/ are both continuing sounds.

1. When saying the sound /l/, air flows out of the mouth around each side of the tongue.

2. When saying the sound /n/, air does not flow out of the mouth. Instead, it flows out of the nose.

1 Look at the pictures to see the differences in tongue position and airflow for the sounds /n/ and /l/.

ten /n/   **tell** /l/

Looking from the side

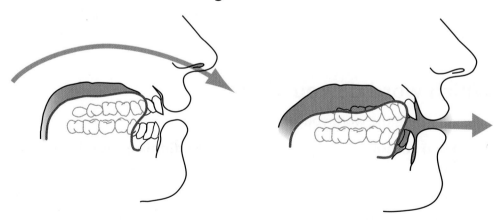

2 Practice the positions for /n/ and /l/. Then whisper the words "ten" and "tell" several times. Pay attention to the difference in air flow for the final sounds.

3 Practice saying "ten" and "tell" out loud.

∩ C Which word do you hear?

1 Listen. Circle the word you hear.

	Final sound				**Beginning sound**	
1.	(pine)	pile		6.	name	lame
2.	cone	coal		7.	nice	lice
3.	main	mail		8.	knife	life
4.	when	well		9.	niece	lease
5.	tune	tool		10.	not	lot

2 Practice saying the words you circled.

∩ D The sound combinations /nd/ and /ld/

Each of the following words ends in the sound combination **/nd/** or **/ld/**.

Listen and repeat each pair of words. Be careful to say the **/n/** and **/l/** sounds clearly.

/nd/	**/ld/**
find	filed
phoned	fold
trained	trailed
mind	mild
spend	spelled
found	fouled

Part 4   /θ/ and /t/

∩ A Listening to /θ/ and /t/

1 Listen to the final sound in each of these words.

bath	bat	both	boat

2 Listen to the beginning sound in each of these words.

thank	tank	thought	taught

Saying /θ/ and /t/

The sound /θ/ as in "bath" is a continuing sound, and the sound /t/ as in "bat" is a sound that stops.

1 Look at the pictures of /θ/ and /t/ below and notice how the air flows out of the mouth for /θ/, but stops inside the mouth for /t/.

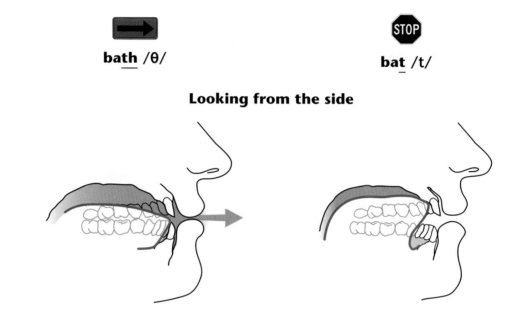

bath /θ/   bat /t/

Looking from the side

Looking to the front

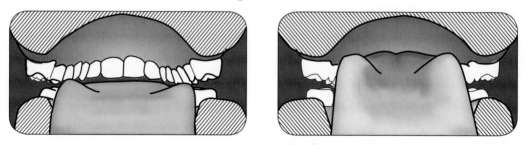

2 When saying /θ/, your tongue is flat. The tip of your tongue touches your lower front teeth.

1. Practice. Feel the air moving over your tongue and teeth as you say the continuing sound /θ/.

2. Now press your tongue on the bump near your teeth. This bump goes all around the roof of your mouth. Now the air cannot flow out. This will make the stopping sound /t/.

∩C Which word do you hear?

1 Listen. Circle the word you hear.

1. (bath)   bat
2. both   boat
3. booth   boot
4. faith   fate
5. Ruth   root
6. math   mat

2 Practice saying the words you circled.

Credits

Illustrations

Judith Alderman: 54 (*looking to the front*), 63 (*looking to the front*), 75 (*looking to the front*), 103 (*looking to the front*), 109 (*looking to the front*), 111, 134, 135, 141 (*looking to the front*), 144 (*looking to the front*); **Judy B. Gilbert:** 38, 39, 41; **Adam Hurwitz:** xi, 4, 12 (*hands*), 14, 15 (*hands*), 29, 30 (*hands*), 34, 45, 49, 54 (*looking down*), 57 (*hands*), 63 (*looking down*), 75 (*looking down, from the side*), 87 (*hands*), 90, 92, 93, 103 (*looking from the side*), 108, 109 (*looking down*), 126, 129, 136, 137, 139, 141 (*looking from the side*), 142, 144 (*looking from the side*); **Chris Reed:** 2, 3, 5, 6, 7, 9, 10, 12 (*top*), 13, 15 (*top*), 17, 19, 20, 21, 22, 23, 25, 26, 30 (*furniture, newspaper*), 31, 33, 40, 43, 46, 47, 50, 51, 52, 57 (*bottom*), 58, 61, 66, 67, 71, 74, 78, 80, 81, 82, 83, 87 (*buildings*), 89, 91, 96, 97, 106, 113, 114, 117, 120, 122, 124

Photo

iii ©Tetra Images/Getty Images

Class and Assessment Audio CD Theme Music

"Lone Jack to Knob Noster" by Jack Rummel from his CD, *Lone Jack: The Ragtime of Today.*

Apple, iPad, iPhone, and iPod touch are trademarks of Apple Inc., registered in the U.S. and other countries. App Store is a service mark of Apple Inc., registered in the U.S. and other countries.